Long Road
To The Manse

Long Road
To The Manse

Gerald Gossage

To Garry & Karen,

With good wishes for 2008

Gerald Gossage

Bloomington, IN   authorHOUSE®   Milton Keynes, UK

AuthorHouse™
1663 Liberty Drive, Suite 200
Bloomington, IN 47403
www.authorhouse.com
Phone: 1-800-839-8640

AuthorHouse™ UK Ltd.
500 Avebury Boulevard
Central Milton Keynes, MK9 2BE
www.authorhouse.co.uk
Phone: 08001974150

This book is a work of non-fiction. Unless otherwise noted, the author and the publisher make no explicit guarantees as to the accuracy of the information contained in this book and in some cases, names of people and places have been altered to protect their privacy.

First published by AuthorHouse 11/4/2006

ISBN: 1-4259-5800-1 (sc)

Printed in the United States of America
Bloomington, Indiana

This book is printed on acid-free paper.

A Note
from the Author

It was in a raging Heat-Wave on the 12th July 1924, that a mother looked for the first time on her new infant, and yelled tenderly "Ahhhr!!". And the author was reluctantly accepted into a loving family. They had to be loving, for I had such a mass of black hair on my head no baby comb would touch it.

My Father had left the first world war behind with lung trouble and was told to find work outdoors or he would not live long, so after several efforts, he turned his passionate hobby of gardening into a daily living, so we did well in the Spring and Summer but woe to us if the Winter was hard.

Sydenham, in South East London was a quiet and pleasant area of Kent then, near enough for easy access to the City, but almost country side.

I grew up in a world of horse drawn traffic with exciting new forms of transport like the first omnibuses and Southern Rail steam trains, and later the electric system. Trams in the middle of the main streets, and milk delivered to the door in large churns from which was measured into your jug on the door step a gill or pint.

Shop keepers stood behind their counters and were subservient and keen to serve you. And the policeman who saw me across the road to school usually had an apple in his pocket for those who were good.

Like most people in those days my parents went to church every Sunday, my only brother was in the choir, and God and The Church became my greatest joy, and has remained so ever since.

I have always had appallingly ill health so I left school at fourteen from the bottom of the class, and was of little use to employers, I was also sure that I could do something special for society and God with my life, so years were lost looking for what I was supposed to do.

Did I make it ? you will have to read this book to find out, and if you are still not sure, get my next book "Long Road Of Miracles". People tell me that you will enjoy both books.

Chapter 1.

"They go to and fro in the evening, grin like a dog, and run about through the city." What a strange thing to sing in church! But there I was standing in the choir stalls of this cathedral like church of Holy Trinity, Sydenham, in South East London, singing just that.

Looking at the congregation I wondered just what spiritual uplift they had received from singing this verse of Psalm 59: There was old Miss Pattrick near the front, I couldn't imagine that she had ever 'grinned like a dog' in her life! And some of the other old dears didn't seem the kind of people that were even likely to 'go to or fro in the evening', more like bed at 9 pm I thought.

But if only I could have known it, those words were going to be a pretty good description of my life over the following few years, I would adventure to and fro in my native London, and often grin at the funny situations I would be thrown into.

Now I was just a youngster in revolt, not long into my teens and still looking like a small school boy. I arrogantly felt amazed at the ignorance of the adult world I saw all around me. I felt determined to put the world right, and was currently starting with reforming the Church of England Creed.

How could they say Sunday by Sunday "I believe in the Holy Catholic Church?" I thought, when we were all Church of England and had nothing to do with the Roman Catholics. How could they talk about "The Communion of Saints?". Everyone knew that the saints were in heaven in their long robes and halos, why would they want to take Holy Communion? These vicars and bishops just hadn't thought it all out: That kind of ignorance was all right for the past, but now they would have to put them right.

The Psalm now came to an end with the 'Gloria', and the Amen; but such was my critical mood, that the service continued with more of my bodily presence than my mental one. I wondered, was there anything at all in this world that didn't need changing?

I thought about my home and parents, and although I was in a mood to find fault with everyone, I had to confess that my parents were great. They would do anything for me; They had high standards, but they did live up to them. They didn't just send me to church as most parents seemed to, they went to church with me, and God meant everything to them.

One of my earliest happy memories was from the age of three, and being taken every Sunday evening to church, sitting in pew thirteen at Christ Church, Forest Hill; I would gaze at the stained glass window most of the time, but I waited for the moment when we would all pray; then I would look at my mother through my cupped hands and see the radiant expression on her face as she silently talked to 'her Lord'. She really knew Him! And I felt I wanted to know Him like that too. In a strange way, I had loved her Jesus then, but slowly over the years He had changed to be 'My Jesus'.

How strange you may think, to take a small boy of such a tender age to an evening service and expect him to sit still!. Yet I did sit still, because mother explained to me that this was what my parents wanted to do; they explained that they did everything for me during the week but that hour was theirs, this is what they wanted to do and I was to just sit quietly; I was to read my book, or cuddle up during the sermon, but be quiet and good to please them. So I did.

I reckoned that I could do that one small thing for them. Although I often spent the time thinking about how we could run my brother's train set around the church pew blocks, and just where the stations would be. I would have fun thinking what that whiskered old man would think if a coal train ran past his pew, or how the old ladies would react to the Flying Scotsman rushing past their feet.

As I grew up 'being religious' earned me a lot of stick from the other boys at school I recall. "Must be someone holy living up there" one boy had scoffed, looking up at my bedroom window and seeing my cross in the window. I went red and felt dreadful. But that cross had a story that I would never tell the boys.

My Aunt had come to visit us from Bristol, and had given us sixpence each to spend in Woolworths; My cousin had bought an aeroplane, and I had bought that crucifix. "You can't play with that" cousin Stuart had said. "I know, but I want it" I had said. "It'll help me to be good". Funny kid I must have been. I feel embarrassed even now as I tell of it.

That cross became part of my early prayers, I shared my boyish sorrows and good times in front of it. I cleaned and repainted it every year; and that went on all through child-hood. No I could never tell the boys what that cross meant to me, perhaps I could not understand it myself.

My only brother, Reg, was nearly nine years older than I, and in some ways more like a second father to me. All through my early days he seemed so much more clever than I was, although it never occurred to me that this was because he was so much older, and that one day I would catch him up.

Reg was in our church choir, so I wanted to be in the choir too; But they said what they always seemed to say to me, "You are too young". On my sixth birthday I had gone all out to convince my parents that I was old enough to join: Finally they said "If the Vicar and the Choirmaster say you can join the choir, you can."

The Vicar was easy, I thought, and he was! But the choir-master was a daunting figure and I was scared stiff even to ask. Summoning all my courage next Sunday, I walked up to him and spoke to him, and was told to come to see him after the Tuesday choir practice.

The audition started with my arriving far too early. Something I was to do all through my life. I sat in the vestry listening to the boys singing in the church, and finally they came tumbling out. After a silent lonely wait which seemed an hour but was probably three minutes, the great man appeared in the doorway with "Come along!".

My mouth was now dry, and I was shaking like a leaf, I was asked to sing scales up and down to 'Loo' 'La' and 'Ah'. I was questioned about the pointing of Psalms, which, having being schooled by my brother I was able to answer with con-fidence, and finally I was invited to sing a hymn of my own choosing. My throat was dry with nervous tension, and as it finished I knew that I could have done much better.

There was a long pause. If the Choirmaster was satisfied, he showed no sign of it. I waited, I prayed in my mind, and hoped desperately. Finally he rubbed his chin saying "I don't think we would have a cassock and surplice to fit someone as small as you."

My face beamed with delight, "My Mother is wonderful at things like that, she could alter one, really she could". There was something of a smile there, then he patted me on the head "all right then". and I was IN.

From that day on I almost lived at the church, on Sundays and whenever I could during the week. In fact that applied to any church, and my parents were known to make detours so that we did not pass a church, for I was certain to demand to go in, and they were all always open in those days. As time went on I had worked up to chief choir boy, soloist, librarian and alms bearer, (the one carrying the big collection plate)

And now I was the Choir member with my voice broken, being told to sit there and do nothing until the voice came back as either bass or tenor. Perhaps it was this change in routine that brought about the restlessness and questioning that I now experienced.

My attitude toward God had grown stronger during boyhood, and it had come to a climax one day when sitting in school. Our teacher had read about some particular saint of old, who stood up for God and for right. I remember saying to myself "Cor! how smashing, I'm going to be like that". I reasoned that if I trusted God and stood up for the right in life, as this saint had, I should please God, and that there could be no higher goal in life than just that. Sitting at that school desk I had told God that I would do whatever He wanted me to do, if He would only make me like that saint.

Now three years later, and having moved house, and to another church, I was still trying to fulfil that pledge, and waiting for a miracle around every next corner.

If I had known then just how many corners I would have to turn before miracles came I might have been most disheartened, and maybe weakened in my resolve.

Now, standing there in church, I was brought back from my day dreaming by the church 'settling down' to the climax of worship.. 'The Sermon!'. The lights were lowered, seats creaked, people made themselves comfortable, and small choir boys practised the art of unwrapping sweets without making a sound.

In our church everyone paid attention during the sermon, not just for the words of wisdom, for, I had to admit the vicar's sermons were helpful, but also because this vicar was unpredictable and might do almost anything, and no one wanted to miss the lunchtime conversation piece.

From the copious folds of his cassock and surplus he might produce some curious item as a visual aid. He might come out with a remark which would startle a wandering mind back to attention... like "Don't doze off through this..." or "If you are the one that hasn't been listening, take this thought home with you.."

Once I remember that his voice grew quieter and quieter, followed by a pause, and then a loud bang on the pulpit "Wake up.. to this gem.." he cried.

Then there was the time when he broke into several not very tuneful verses of "Ring the bells of heaven, there is joy today" to the disapproval of the Organist-choirmaster who shook his head and 'tut-tutted'. Believe me, our sermons were never boring, in fact we often heard laughter in our church; And why not! Sometimes the laughter was unintentional, and I still laugh over the event of 'The Angel's Wing'.

The Angel in question was a beautifully carved wooden angel, one of many which decorated the pulpit stairway. The carved pulpit stood high above the congregation, and was reached by a circular flight of stairs, the hand rail hidden from view by a flight of wooden angels with wings outspread.

On this Sunday morning, the vicar having concluded his sermon, announced the next hymn number, the people thumbed through their hymn books finding the place, and the organ started to play the tune over, as a usual introduction.

As I watched from my place in the choir, the vicar turned and started to descend the pulpit steps. As his hand grasped the rail, the sleeve of his surplus enfolded the top carved angel with outstretched wings. He took the first step downward, the surplice tightened. The second step caused him to flick his arm as he felt his sleeve tighten; this caused the angel's head to pop up from under the white sleeve as if playing 'Peep - Bo'.

As he took his third step down his hand slid downward also, 'Surely he must feel it' I thought. One more step down and the sleeve was pulled to its limit! Something had to happen! Would it slip off? Or would it tear the material? In taking the next step he felt the restriction to his arm, and he gave an impatient tug. SNAP! The angel lost its wing! and as if by catapult it sailed high into the air, across the chancel. It just missed a small choir boy in the front stalls, but it struck a Bald headed Bass named Bagshaw.

He, forgetting where he was, let out a cry of pain and startled surprise, just at that moment of hush that comes between the organ playing the tune and the people starting to sing. Several looked up at the sound, but failing to locate it, started to sing; while the irate Mr Bagshaw was waving a hymn book in one hand and now rubbing his bald head with the other. Looking wildly round and making comments that nobody heard or seemed to notice. I shall never forget that comical look of pain, surprise, and anger.

By the direction of his looks he seemed convinced that 'one of those choir boys were up to their tricks again'.

It was time for me to hide behind my hymn book so that no one should see me laughing so much that the tears were streaming down my face.

The memory of that look of startled surprise on the Bagshaw face caused me to laugh for weeks after. It did not occur to me that the poor man might be hurt, but as he left the vestry that morning I noticed a sizable bump on the Bagshaw bald head. Strangely no one seemed to notice or to say anything, not even the injured party, and I wondered just what he would say to his wife when he got home.

Later I found the angel's wing behind the choir stalls, picking it up I put it in the pulpit for someone to find and glue back on to the one winged angel.

Carved wooden angels are one thing, but what about real angels? Do real angels watch over us? Perhaps my brother Reg and I owe our lives to the watchfulness of angels, I don't know, but there was a time in our childhood when we both nearly lost our lives: We were very nearly gassed to death while we slept.

The house in which I was born had been built as a local hospital and had fifteen very large rooms. When a new children's hospital was built at Lower Sydenham, the old one was sold off and made into three flats. My parents rented the basement and the ground floor flats, subletting the basement to tenants; who, always pleaded that they were too poor to pay their rent.

As was usual in those days, the rooms were lit by coal-gas which was supplied through a 'shilling in the slot' meter, On the nearly fateful night, I had been sent off to bed first, as the youngest, my brother being sent off later. He had received permission to read in bed for half an hour and had lit the gas light in our bedroom. Before his half an hour was up however, he had fallen asleep over his book with the light still burning.

Sometime later the gas in the meter ran out, and so out went all the lights. Father, down stairs, placed another shilling in the meter, and the gas supply was resumed. Re lighting their gas lamp down stairs they thought no more about it. But as no one was awake in our bedroom the gas just hissed through without being lit.

Our parents came to bed shortly after, they noticed that there was no light shining under our bedroom door and concluded that my brother had put his light out sometime ago and was tucked down for the night.

Later on I was heard making whimpering noises, and as I had not been well of late Father came into the room, picked me up, and took me into their bed, but being half asleep and having no sense of smell he didn't smell the gas that filled our room.

However the opening and closing of our bedroom door had sent enough gas out to finally reach my mother's nose who finally aroused herself and came to investigate where the gas smell was coming from.

At once she threw open our bedroom windows, turned the gas off, and roused father, who kept us from going into a sleep from which we would never have awakened.

They could not awaken my brother and I remember that they lifted him outside to the front lawn and, between the two of them, made him walk up and down until he woke up.

Three things remain in my memory about that event. One, all of us were up all night, and it seemed a very very long night. Two, we both kept being sick and it was a nasty green colour. And three, it was near to the season of Christmas, and Mother was so delighted that we were alive, that she went out and spent all the money they had saved for Christmas on gifts for us, to show her thankfulness. That part we rather enjoyed!

Christmas! Ah now, there's a season! It was then, and always has been since, the most wonderful season of the year for me.. We mostly made our own decorations in those days of the late twenties, early thirties, paper chains being put all around the house. Money was always in short supply for us, as it was for most families: but the excitement was built up, family plans were discussed, secret discussion took place about what we could give as presents, and of the coming of Father Christmas, Oh how that magic thrilled us. I don't think it has ever really left me.

I can still feel the excitement of waking up on Christmas mornings while it was still dark, braving the bitter cold outside the blankets,(no central heating in those days) and feeling for the stocking tied to the foot of the brass bedstead of my bed, a long stocking of mother's, full of bulges and lumps and paper wrappings that rustled, sheer magic!

The bedside candle would be lit and in it's golden glow we would thrill to each new surprise. I was always a little annoyed to find the usual apple and orange in the toe of the stocking: didn't Father Christmas know that this was the one time of year that we had fruit like this downstairs?

If Mum and Dad knew we were awake we would be called into their bed, and they would try to keep us warm and share our delights. Those were the days when bedroom fireplaces only had a fire lit if someone was ill, so there was always a great haste to get down to the warm kitchen to play with our new toys. Our main toys were nearly always tin plate, I had a passion for clockwork cars or trains, We also had wooden toys, often home made, and books of course. My brother, Reg, was very keen on stamps and trains, and these were usually his presents. Later he also had an old gramophone and got gifts of the old 78rpm records.

As soon as I was old enough I also had a train set given me for Christmas. I recall removing the paper wrapping and seeing a wonderful picture of a real train in full steam on the box. I don't quite know what I expected, but I felt a bit cheated when the inside revealed a stamped out tin train set, (as always 'made in Germany from old tins'). But it did run around on it's little circle of track till it's spring wound down.

My brother and I had a kind of pact after that, we would build up our railway and play together. So this meant we had extra track,, and straight track, rolling stock or porters for birthday and Christmas presents, and sometimes we spent our pocket money choosing small station items, or loads for wagons. The smell of those cardboard boxes and oiled clockwork trains lingers still with a magic delight.

In the warm weather Reg would take me down the road to the railway footbridge where we could watch the real Southern Railway steam trains coming and going at Forest Hill Station. Roaring beneath the footbridge we stood on, covering us with steam that smelt delightful; and listening to a brother's words of wisdom and he gave me engine names, numbers, and wheel base details.

During holidays we would run our toy train track from one room to another, sending trains with written notes, or sweets, or unusual items of freight. The glorious day when we both caught measles brought us two weeks of playing together and the railway stayed on the floor without orders to "pack it all away now!"

When playing in the garden one day Reg had the great idea of building a tunnel under the garden for our trains.

We wanted something between us to block our view of each other, so it was decided to dig a tunnel underneath the gooseberry bushes. We tunnelled from each end shoring up with wood and cardboard and finally had a wooden plank running underneath the bush, we had a good tunnel. Sliding our straight lengths of track through, we were soon running a train service which used a real tunnel. Trains went down into the tunnel at great speed but it was always doubtful if the clockwork spring would be strong enough to pull the train up and into the open air the other side.

The game came to an abrupt halt with "Look out! Dad's coming!". His feet were crunching up the long sweep of the front gravel drive as he returned from work, and we knew he would see us in this, his 'kitchen garden' at the side of the house, so we hid ourselves quickly.

As soon as he passed, to ascend the house front steps we rushed to put the garden back to normal. Whipping out the track and wooden planks we filled in the holes and carried our trains indoors.

Dad, always a very keen gardener, soon appeared in the garden, closely followed by Mum who was probably keen to protect us if we had been up to mischief. He saw the gooseberry bushes, "Look at this, Mum" he cried, viewing the cave in of a recent tunnel "Those blessed cats have been at it again". A Mum and two boys hastily turned away and tried not to show him our mirth.

Before I was three I started to have nose bleeds, and Oh boy! were they nose bleeds! Once started, it did not know how to stop. For hours and sometimes for days I just bled. I had cold keys dropped down my back, my feet put into hot water, The poor old nose was plugged with wadding, and cotton wool, soaked in everything from Witch Hazel to Vinegar.

Doctors could not stop it, hospitals plugged it, but it didn't stop for long. Great Ormond Street Hospital in London gave me papers to say that I had Haemophilia, which later proved to be wrong, As Russian Royalty suffered from this, the doctor looked at me and said "You must have blue blood in your veins sonny". I told him "I've only seen red so far sir". "Let me know if it turns blue". He said.

I was told not to rush about or exert myself in any way. From that day on I was excused all games and P.T. at school and had to lead a very quiet life.

Exercise, The heat of summer, or excitement would bring on a nose bleed, and this was to go on well into my twenties. I was constantly told "don't run, you'll make your nose bleed". "don't get excited, you'll make your nose bleed".

Many an hour was spent flat on my back under the school black board in class, swallowing blood, while the chalk dust fell on me from the board above like fine snow whenever the teacher wrote on it; After a while I would rush out and be sick, and then start all over again.

Many an outing was ruined because of my nose bleeds, many happy occasions had sad endings, and I had to be very careful not to upset any other boy because it might end in a fight and a punch on the nose!

Once one of the boys did punch me on the nose and I was away from school for a week. My Mother went to the school playground and found out which boy had punched me and she quietly chatted to him all through play time explaining the situation. After this the boy, Bernard, became my champion and if any boy wanted to fight me Bernard pleaded and explained for me, and if all else failed he fought them for me. He was to remain a good friend until we were well into our twenties.

As I was also very good at regularly catching 'Flu, colds and every other ailment going around. I lost much time away from school, and usually spent my school days 'catching up with the others', but I never did seem to achieve even that. At the end of each term I always got three 'excellents' on school reports 'Scripture, Punctuality and Conduct', other than that it seemed I was a failure!

Perhaps I might be forgiven therefore for growing up a little shy and detached from others who could do everything that I could not do, and who seemed to know everything that I did not know; and even be forgiven for sometimes being a little goodie goodie! I could never swim, play cricket or football or join it energetic games, or be one of the boys.

There were compensations, however. There was a dear old man who always sat in a special pew at church, and always went to church on Sunday in a top hat, an item rapidly going out of fashion. He befriended three of us choir boys and took us each in turn to either the Penge Empire or the Lewisham Hippodrome where we saw all the variety acts of the day. I suppose he was lonely and enjoyed our company, he was always good fun to be with and he gave us so much pleasure and also a view into a world that we would never have seen other wise.

A major problem loomed ever closer with my coming fourteenth birthday. Unless a child was very brainy or had parents who were rich enough to send their child to further education,, age fourteen was the time when everyone left school.

Most boys knew what they wanted to do in life by this time, many followed their father in what he did, others wanted to be an engine driver or similar. I did not know what I wanted to do or even what I could do. I didn't seem academically acceptable for clerical work, neither was I able to do manual work because of my blood condition.

My Mother and I were invited to attend a meeting at the school which would seek to help pupils to obtain employment. We waited our turn to be called before the committee, noticing the happiness of most of the other boys and parents who appeared to be fixed up with just what they wanted, and finally our turn came.

Entering the room I saw that my vicar was seated among these worthies, so also was my headmaster, both knew me well and had shown an interest in me, I began to feel a little easier, perhaps they would suggest something suitable as a career. There was much shifting of papers, and I was asked my name more than once. At last the chairman said "Ah! Oh yes" in a meaningful tone. Then slowly he spoke as he read the papers "There doesn't seem to be anything.. er.. outstanding.. er... what work did you have in mind?" Peering over his glasses he said in a more conversational tone "What are you going to do for a living sonny, er?"

I took courage from his smile "I would like to know how to go about getting into the Ministry of The Church ,Sir". I asked. There was a pause; they looked at me.. a very little boy with no scholarship; anything less like a potential vicar would be hard to imagine; They looked at one another, and then they all laughed. I felt that they were laughing at me, and my cheeks flushed.

It seemed reasonable to me. I had been Baptised, and Confirmed, was a member of the Church of England. I was at a church school, had spent most of my young life in the church's service, a good living lad, from a good home, and I wanted to serve God. Why should they find it so funny?

"What do you think, vicar?" The chairman looked to the vicar for a lead. "I should think that he is probably attracted by the vestments". came the reply. My Mother was not going to let it stop there "How high is the academic standard for the ministry?" "Very high indeed" the vicar smiled, "I doubt if the boy who came top of the class this year could make it, and your boy is very near the bottom you know". "Quite impossible!". And nothing else was said about it. After some ramblings it was suggested that I should learn to ride a bike and apply to some local shop as an errand boy; With that, the interview was terminated.

When we were outside, my Mother, ever the comforter, soon had me smiling again "Better give up the idea of being a vicar and try for a job as a Bishop" she smiled, "You could give that vicar the sack then".

Then, turning to me with some earnestness "Do you really think God wants you to go into the church?" she asked. "Yes" I beamed "It's the only thing I really do want". "Then I think one day you will," she encouraged "But you will have to work harder than you have ever worked before, you have such a long way to catch up in your schooling".

"Remember this!" she urged "If you are sure you have to do something, don't let anything or anyone put you off".

I hope that all Mothers are as wise as mine!

On the walk home we discussed whether, if I were a Bishop I could put a stop to "Those Bells"!

"Those Bells" were the vicars latest 'Great Idea'. We had moved to a little semi-detached house which was right opposite the church of Holy Trinity, Sydenham, where we had now transferred our membership, and the bells were driving us and our neighbours mad.

To put you in the picture; when Holy Trinity Church was built, most of the population lived behind it and so a single bell had been housed at the rear of the church, this had successfully called the faithful to church each Sunday for years. Then, around 1934/5 a new estate of semis were built in front of the church, and the church now served these houses also. The vicar had this idea to have bells ringing from the front of the church; so within his vestry at the front of the church, he installed a record playing device consisting of a pick-up, turntable, amplifier and records. Upon the flat vestry roof above, he erected a large black horn-type loudspeaker which was fitted onto to movable supports sticking out of a black wooden box; this box concealed an electric motor which moved the horn-loudspeaker backward and forwards so that the sound could be sprayed over the estate. Recordings of bells and hymns played from the vestry would be amplified to reach the whole area.

During the installation period we were blasted with very loud snippets of Bow Bells, and we learned to play 'guess the tune' as odd bits of hymn tunes came roaring through in one or two second bursts, amid crackles and pops as wires were fiddled with within the vestry.

Living opposite the church we watched the antics of the vicar and his sons, climbing ladders, trailing cables, and shouting orders to each other. When ever the vicar looked across to us he would just beam a smile. He was very happy it seemed! When we met him he would apologise for 'these times of testing!'.

As work progressed we were submitted to longer periods of enforced listening, for it became impossible to listen to the radio or anything else indoors while the church system bellowed at us. The vicar then toured the area to see how far the sound travelled at certain volume levels.

On Sunday he assured us that "It will be just wonderful when it is finished". So we put up with the 'trials that beset us'.

Completion date did finally arrive. There was a service of Dedication for The Bells, and with great ceremony and prayers they offered the system to God. Those Bells were now part of the church.

From that day onward our small corner of Sydenham was blasted awake with bells every Sunday morning at ten minutes to seven for Holy Communion, and if anyone got off to sleep again after that, they could count on being aroused by a second performance for the eight o'clock Communion, and there was no 'Snooze button' to turn it off.

At eleven and six-thirty we had "popular" (or not so popular) hymns, followed by more Bow Bells to remind the population that they had just five minutes to be in their pew or the service would start without them.

As we were leaving church one Sunday soon after, the vicar asked "What do you think of those bells now?" My father, ever polite to vicars replied "Oh I'm sure we shall get used to them in time." This was plainly not what the vicar had expected. "I don't think you have quite the right idea about them." he smiled "The hymns are to help us all to higher thoughts as we prepare for worship, and the bells are a gentle reminder to come to God's house, not to Be Got Used To".

After this, whenever we were startled by the sudden barrage of noise from over the road we would comment "It's only a gentle reminder of something!".

Then came Christmas Eve! All over the estate quiet preparations for the coming day were peacefully pursued and finally children were slumbering, no doubt dreaming of the coming of Father Christmas.

Then suddenly they were jerked back to wakefulness and excited expectations from bulging stockings by the loud reminder that 'On Christmas Night All Christians Sing'; it was the call to the Midnight Service. Parents rushed to their offspring, putting toys back into stockings with assurances that although Santa HAD been, there were, hopefully, seven hours or so before they would be brought back again from dreamland by 'O Come All Ye Faithful', on Christmas morning.

At home, we took the view, that we had known friends who lived close to railway lines, and some whose house was on a main road with noisy trams grinding down the hill, and they had all got so used to it that they didn't notice it. If they could get used to noise, so would we in the end.

On Saturdays, wedding couples paid extra for the 'joy' of standing on the lawn beneath the sound of Bow Bells to have their photos taken, and all weekly services were now marked by the records.

"In time we shall get used to them" we sighed!

Then there were Sundays when the horn got stuck in one position, which was great if it was pointing away from us, but overpowering if it stuck facing us.

Following this there was the first Sunday that the needle got stuck in one groove of the record, and those outside were treated to a 90 second hiccough, while those of us inside the church were treated to the amusing sight of the vicar trying to make great haste with slow dignity from the back of the church to the front vestry, to effect a cure.

As the novelty wore off the vicar would forget to keep a listening ear to the hymn or bells being played and they would end in seemingly endless scuffing noises that only the ending of an old 78 RPM record can make. When at last someone arrived to give it some attention the pickup would be put back onto the record anywhere, and the result was a restart in the middle of a line of a hymn.

As the records became worn by constant use, the bells and hymn sounds coming from the loudspeaker were increasingly lost in a background of noise as the needle scuffed it's way through the worn out grooves.

Then, there followed a few blissful weeks when the system broke down altogether, and finally the Church Magazine announced that the use of the system would be discontinued.

However, 'Those Bells' were dedicated to the church, and under ecclesiastical law could not be removed, or so we were told. So there, hanging over the grey stone battlements, remained the horn on it's black box; drooping more sadly as the days went by; there to await the Day of Judgment or destruction by the elements, which ever might come first. When war came in 1939 no church bells could be rung, except to warn the population of an enemy invasion. My mother remarked," We can truthfully say that the last thing in all the world we want to hear again is 'Those Blessed Bells'". And we never did hear them again.

Chapter 2.

London was only twelve miles away, and the local Ministry of Labour, or Labour Exchange as it was called, offered me my first job. I made my way to The Victoria School of Motoring, in Pimlico Road, Victoria. The business was owned by two brothers who had two Vauxhall 12.6 cars, and spent their days teaching people to drive.

"We want a bright lad who can sweep the shop in the morning, keep it dusted and tidy, book appointments for driving lessons and be pleasant to the customers". I was told. I knew I could do that! I was engaged to "start next Monday."

The wages were fifteen shillings a week (75p today); It seems unbelievable now, but with that money I could commute by train to London, have lunch each day, give something toward the family income, and still have some spending money in my pocket.

I was an 'office boy', sometimes known as a 'tea boy', I was five foot tall, fresh school-boy complexion, and looking just what I was, a kid from school. But I didn't see it that way: Each day I now mixed with bowler hatted, pinstripe suited city men, and I thought I was one of them. How I hated it when railway porters and others called me 'son' or 'sonny', they probably meant it as a term of endearment, I took it as a personal insult!

Travelling back and forth each day in the train I slowly formed a plan to show everyone that I was 'grown up'. When Saturday came I visited our local 'F.W.Woolworth 3d & 6d Store' (nothing cost more than six pence, two and a half pence today) and I bought a proper man's pipe. Monday morning saw me walking to the station with the pipe in my mouth. I was a man! Most commuters didn't notice I existed, but those who did seemed to give a patronizing smile, and once one person nudged his friend and pointed to me and they both laughed. I wondered why! A solution came to me that my pipe had a clean shiny inside, to the bowl, it had never been used for smoking! So I hid it in my pocket.

My Father smoked cigarettes so on reaching home I slit open some of his butt ends and filled my pipe with real tobacco, now I was ready to go to the office like a man.

Somehow I was still dissatisfied, it occurred to me that a pipe filled with tobacco was better than an empty one, but if it had 'burnt ash' in it, it would look better. That evening I slipped from the house after tea and made my way to the garden shed armed with a box of matches. I lit up, Ugh! it was nasty, what did these smokers see in it? My mouth went dry, and most of the tobacco burnt through quickly, so I put in some more from dad's butt ends, I lit it again; that looked better, but what were those little stars jumping about above me? I rushed outside and brought back my tea.

For a few days I went to work with my pipe but didn't smoke it. Then I found out that the inside of a new pipe should be scraped so I got my pen knife and scraped the bowl of the pipe, filled it with more butt ends and lit up. Once more I saw stars and ended up behind the shed.

After more thought I came to the conclusion that smoking father's cigarette ends was the problem! I bought some cheap pipe tobacco and tried again. I was more sick than ever, even though I tried it several times. (Well you couldn't waste real tobacco!) I now knew that I could not smoke a pipe.

One morning crammed in the train compartment like sardines I was pressed against someone's brief case and the pipe broke in half, that seemed to be the end of the matter.

Woodbine cigarettes were 2d (two old pence) for five so I bought some, they tasted horrid so I only smoked them in front of people that I wanted to impress. Soon the habit took hold of me so I obtained permission from Dad to smoke, and when later I had a cigarette case and lighter as birthday presents I was hooked as a smoker.

The smoking habit was to grow until I had nicotine fingers, bad breath, and it took most of my weekly pocket money. I was to try hard to give it up again and again but I would be in my late twenties before I would find the secret and be free of it for ever. How I wished I had never started!

My new working life was strange and exciting. Each morning I would leave home and join the crowds going along Girton Road, where we lived at that time, to the Penge East Station. I noticed that men would leave their front door at exactly the same time each day, you could set your watch by them. At each road turning, the commuter stream grew larger. At the station, busses disgorged more, until there was a vast throng surging up the station approach, over the foot bridge, to be joined by still more from other directions the other side. They poured through the double open doors of the station building and onto the platform where trains thundered in one after another, with only a few minutes in between.

Some trains went to Holborn Viaduct Station, others to Victoria, and although the crowd seemed always engrossed in newspapers, or conversation only some late comers, slipping through the barrier at the last moment might ask which train it was.

Trains would roar in, doors would open, bodies would push in, doors would slam, porters would rush up and down checking doors and sometimes throwing their weight against the door of over packed compartments, crammed in standing passengers in order to get them closed. Whistles would blow, a flag waved. and off.

Inside each compartment the two long seats would be filled, plus as many standing passengers who could cram in. Each would try to read a bit of his massive newspaper as the train raced to the next signal and then stopped for the train ahead to clear the section, then race to the next one.

There were not many women commuting in those days, but those who did were always allowed to get in first of course, and those men who had boarded further down the line would usually get up to let a lady sit down: although this did not always happen, for I remember one amusing and embarrassing incident.

Seated among the city gents one morning was a very fat workman: Standing between his out spread knees was a tall beautiful young blonde girl whose arm reached over the man as she held on to the parcel rack above, in her hand she also held a small white ladies handkerchief.

As the train rattled along she dropped her hankie and it landed between the man's legs, in fact on his flies. She saw where it was and didn't know quite what to do about it. A man sitting next to him took in the situation and tried to tell the fat commuter that the young lady had dropped her hankie. He didn't hear, above the roar of the train, so fingers were pointed down to the white lost property still laying on his trouser flies. The fat man looked down, saw the hankie and pushed it in through his flies until it disappeared within his large trousers, turned to the man and said "Thanks mate".

At journey's end the carriage doors would open before the train stopped, and the mass of humanity would pour on to the wooden platform which thundered to their many feet. Through the barrier and out, to radiate like the spokes of a cycle wheel, each man knowing just where he was going. Many of these men had done that same journey all their lives, going to the same office, doing the same things, all day, every day. It would take world war two to break most of them from the rat race.

As for me I was new to it all. At Victoria Station I would be swept along with the crowd until I found my way to the little shop in Pimlico Road where at great expense (Three pounds seventy five pence now) you could take a full course of driving tuition.

Each morning I would wait for the shop to open, then sweep and dust it. People both called in and phoned to enquire about learning to drive, and to book lessons. Most of the driving lessons started from the shop so I had to keep the customers happy while they were waiting for their lesson to start. Where there was a time space between lessons I would put the kettle on and have a cup of tea waiting for the returning instructor.

Life did not always run smoothly, there could be traffic delays, minor and major breakdowns and punctures were more frequent in those days.

One morning one of the brothers, Claud, returned half-way through a lesson with a puncture in the front off side tyre. Normally this would have been changed on the road and other bookings would have run a few minutes late, but on this occasion the same car had returned with a puncture after the first lesson of the day and the spare was still waiting repair in the office.

The bookings were already now ten minutes late and the other car was not due back with it's spare tyre for fifty minutes. Panic!

The car had pulled up on the other side of the busy London road with the client still waiting for the rest of his lesson, which had started ten minutes late anyway. Mr Claud had placed the jack under the car, removed the wheel nuts and now was making his way across the street dodging the traffic with the wheel in his dirty hands.

"Go and get the tyre levers, puncture outfit, rubber solution, valves and every thing else I'll need ". he shouted to me. So off I went to the car, crossing the busy street. Anxious to please and not knowing exactly what to bring I probably brought more than I needed. I turned to re-cross the street with tool roll, tyre levers, puncture repair outfit, french chalk, foot pump etc and on top of the pile lay a giant economy-size tin of rubber solution.

I saw a gap in the traffic and ran across. As I did so the large tin of rubber solution slipped from the top of the pile and landed on the tarmac road with a dull thud. I could do nothing about it, I had both hands full and a van was bearing down upon me. I hastened to the office, dropped my load of tools on the floor and returned to retrieve the rubber solution.

I arrived at the kerb to find no space in the traffic; but there, on the road half way between me the parked car, was the giant economy size tin of rubber solution. The boss joined me at the kerb, but neither of us could find a gap in the onrush of vehicles.

Three or four vehicles missed the tin by inches, one just touched it causing it to roll toward us a little, then stop. Then a big double decker bus bore down toward us, and ran right over it, with a bursting sound and squash! We now witnessed the most amazing sight as ten-thousand tiny threads of rubber shot like a firework display into the air covering everything it touched. In a moment the bus looked as if some giant spider had spun a web from wheels to roof, then it was gone.

A following car hit the pool of pink rubber solution and became instantly gift-wrapped in appearance with a thousand fine threads. Taxi cabs, vans, even a motor cyclist hit the now spreading puddle, covering themselves and each other with silver strands and rubber bands. The lamp post looked like a Christmas Tree draped with tinsel, the phone box on the pavement was a mess. The street and everything that passed through it was coated with millions of strands fine rubber threads. And so were we!.

The boss took me by the shoulders back into the office. "An awful lot of people are going to curse you when they come to clean that lot off" he said "and that is nothing to what I would like to do to you". "Here" he placed some money into my hand "I ought to stop this out of your wages. Go and buy some more rubber solution quick!". "And Gossage... " "Sir?" " DON'T DROP IT!"

Soon after I joined this firm, the brothers thought that they could expand the business. They bought a new car, a Flying Standard Eight, and engaged a new instructor. He was a young fellow and probably good at his job, but did not seem too bright to me. He was now entrusted with the key to the office, to open up each morning, and as my train got me to work early I was usually found outside waiting for him.

On the pavement outside the premises there was a public telephone box, and one rainy morning I took refuge in this box until the little man should arrive. When I saw him coming down the road I had a rather naughty idea. Feeding two pennies into the phone pay box I lifted the receiver and dialled our office number. I could not only hear the ringing tone but also hear the phone ringing inside the office. The fellow approached the door, heard the phone ringing and thrust the key quickly into the lock, rushing to the phone. As he lifted it I replaced my phone and pressed button 'B' to regain my two pence.

"I just missed it" he panted, "The phone was ringing..." and I listened to his story of a possible lost booking.

The next morning I was again waiting for him in the phone box and I gave a repeat performance of yesterday's practical joke. To my surprise he fell for it, rushing in to pick up the phone, and then telling me all about it when I appeared a little later.

Again on the third morning I repeated the exercise, and again he rushed for the instrument only to find the caller ring off. "They ring every morning" he told me "I expect they have to be at work by a certain time and can't hang on, I'll get here early tomorrow".

He did so, and so did I; I expected him to twig what was going on, and I wondered how he would take it when he found out it was me. But he responded just as before: "They just rang off again " he looked puzzled "What can I do?" When the boss came in the little man made quite an issue of the mysterious phone calls "What I can't understand is that I only just miss them every time". he mused "What do you think I should do?". "There's nothing that you can do" the boss replied, then turning to me he gave me a look as he said "I don't suppose it will go on much longer"! I spent a long time wondering just what that look was intended to convey, was it 'You had better stop now' or 'Some mothers do have them don't they?'

The phone never rang again as the little man unlocked the shop door, and he never mentioned it again either, Do you think he ever knew?

Cars had always been one of my passions, although there were not so many about when I was small. I must have been about six or seven when the doctor offered to give me my first ride to the top of the road if I recovered quickly from some illness.

He had a 'Bull-nosed Morris and when he gave me the choice of, in front or in the back I did not appreciate that when the boot was opened it contained what they called a 'dicky' seat. I therefore chose to sit up with the driver. When

I think about it I can still smell the leather interior and the warm engine smell. No modern car smells like it today.

After that whenever I walked around town I would be driving an imaginary car. I never thought that I might one day drive, as such a thing was reserved for rich people in those days, even trade vehicles were mostly horse drawn carts. Imagine my joy then when the boss offered to teach me to drive a little. Of course I was too young to have a licence and too small to drive without cushions, but in the private yard at the side I learned the controls and was shown how to start and stop, There was one day when I did even more than that, but I best say no more about that.

All this helped when three years later I applied for my first driving licence: Because the war was on by then there was no instruction or tests to be had, I recall that when I was let loose on the road with a licence I drove around in first gear because I could not work out how to use the clutch. I used any vehicle that I could persuade the owner to let me borrow and drove around London streets learning as I went.

These were the days before mass car ownership, and in days of petrol rationing, so the streets of London were not busy or as dangerous as today.

It was during the early days of this my first employment that I lived through the shock of puberty. I was later to learn that my parents had asked our vicar to explain the facts of life to me at the time he was preparing me for Confirmation. They thought he had done so, He hadn't! The pain and later experience were a worry and shock. With this experience I also took a little more interest in the opposite sex.

The school of motoring had a branch office, (it was at their home in Wimbledon, although I did not know that at the time.) I was often on the phone to the Branch Office, and looked forward to such communications as the girl on the other end of the line sounded gorgeous, it was not long before I changed from being very nice, to down right flirting and suggesting that we might make a date. She told me she was blonde and attractive and I felt my heart flutter every time she was on the line.

One afternoon the two brothers walked in with a woman they introduced as their older sister, She was tall and on the plump side with straight blonde hair, and looked old enough to be my mother. "We thought it was about time you met her" Mr Claude said "You've spoken often enough to her on the phone". I had never felt so confused and embarrassed in my life, but give them their due they were very kind in that they sent me off to a shop to buy something while they enjoyed their laugh, and when I returned they had gone.

The brothers worked hard to build their business, I felt so proud to see big adverts in Victoria Station recommending people to learn to drive with us. But there was a depression country wide, and London was feeling it badly.

The depression caused my brother Reg to leave the city and join the Royal Air Force as an electrical tradesman, and even I noticed that there were many times during the day when no clients were booked to learn to drive. People could not afford cars, and firms were cutting staff not expanding.

After Christmas Mr Claude took me aside and explained that they could no longer keep me in their employ. He gave me a letter to give my parents explaining the situation and giving me one weeks notice of termination. I treasure still the reference I was given by the brothers, they could not have made it easier for me to find new employment, but on 20th

January 1939 I was out of work after only six months since leaving school.

Once more my Mother asked "What do you want to be in life?" Once more I asked about how I might go into the Christian Ministry. So she found out for me. I was far too young to start college, and before I could go to college I would have to have a high examination standard including Latin. "Ugh!" I said, "I could never study to that level" It seemed that God is not calling in that direction, so I looked for a new job in the columns of our local newspaper. One ad' said:-

'WANTED. a smart lad to learn to be a Display Artist in a large department store. Apply to Walter Cobb Limited.'

I knew Cobbs, the local department store in Sydenham, only a short walk from where I lived. I applied, and was accepted at 12/6d a week,(62p) so it was two shillings and six pence less than before, but with no fares to pay, and lunches at home, I would not lose out. I started my training as a window dresser. A general dogsbody who was there to fetch and carry for the real artists of display.

Cobbs, was typical of the large department stores of the time, they sold everything in small sections of glass counters, and on every floor of the building. With a little class added! Sited along the main road it had many large windows in which the goods for sale were tastefully displayed to attract the public to buy. Each window display was regularly dismantled and redressed, this was the display departments job.

My Mother made for me a small velvet pin cushion with an elastic strip to fit on my wrist, and I was equipped with material overshoes and I started my new career.

On the second day I was there it was decided to dismantle the china and glass window. This posted me outside the window with large wicker baskets in which to pack the china and glass for return to that department.

An experienced display artist entered the window area and started removing tea sets and wine glasses, handing them to me through the doorway. The glass and china items were balanced on small sheets of glass supported by tripods, and while the good lady worked at it she passed instruction to me about how she was doing it. "Start from the top, support the glass while you remove the outside items first" and so on.

I had just got into the rhythm of things when she changed it all. "Now!" she breathed, emerging from the window, "You get in there and finish it off". She swept out and I entered and looked around to see how to proceed.

She could only just have got out of earshot when tragedy struck. I had forgotten to put on my overshoes with the result that my shoe pulled the floor covering just enough to move a towering mass of crockery and send it tumbling, I bent to save it and struck my bottom on another part of the display behind me and that also crashed down. The noise in that confined space was terrifying! Everything seemed to crash together, and when it stopped my ears were ringing.

I stood quite still and waited. I expected people to come rushing in. No one came! Surely they must have heard that new kid dismantling the china and glass window? Nothing happened! The store was going about it's business of serving customers. I stood and looked at the debris around me, I looked for breakages, there must be loads! I could see nothing broken. With great care I removed each part of a wrecked dinner service and took it out to the wicker baskets, not a chip or break could I find. Other items, ornaments, glass ware, Not A Chip or Break! I finished the job, and no one said a word, I went home for lunch, my nerves were still in tatters. "Enjoying your new job?" Mum smiled? "Yes thank you it's smashing!" I grinned. "I finished off the china and glass this morning".

Over the next three or four weeks I tried to get interested in my new career, I read magazines for display artists, I went looking at the work of other window dressers, I did all I could to learn the arts of the trade, and I prayed about it. "I'm only fourteen" I told myself "I've time to learn everything about this work and end up working in one of the big London stores". But then came my black day of testing and I failed miserably!

It was mid morning when I was told to take out window No.5. all by myself. This window turned out to be a simple fashion display with dummies showing women clothing. Here was a simple job that even I could do without smashing anything, I need have no fear. I had been taught how to unpin blouses without damaging the material and I soon had these neatly folded and boxed ready to take to the department.

I now tackled the dummies, hoping to finish by lunch time. I took two half dummies from the window and undressed them outside, I then started on the full sized dummies. It was at this moment that a number of children I knew from my old school came past on their way home for lunch. "Cor! look there's Gossage!". one called, and in a flash I had an audience. 'Ignore them' I thought, but there was nothing to do in the window now but undress two female dummies.

I did not want to do this in front of these children who were already calling at me through the plate glass, so I made toward the door, but my way was barred by the form of the Managing Director himself talking to one of the buyers. I returned to what seemed like a cage in the zoo, and I was the exhibit. How would I perform?

The dummy nearest me was too heavy to lift and to make matters worse it's back was close to the wall. The only way I could see to remove the bra it was wearing was to put my arms round it from the front and feel how it might be fastened. Somehow it didn't dawn on me that from the outside of the window it would look as if I were embracing a "semi-nude" female figure, and the action was greeted with cat calls, whistles, and rude remarks from the other side of the glass.

I searched for pins, ribbons, or clips, my fingers pushed, pulled and fiddled but when you are only fourteen you don't know much about the methods of fixing women's clothes and I could not remove the bra. I came up for air and looked round at the audience; to my horror the small group of boys had grown, there was a sizable number of adults too now, some just looking, others grinning.

I looked for some other task. The other dummy was dressed in ladies pyjamas, I thought that this would be easier.

Pretending that the crowd was not there I moved to the other dummy and, having been shown how, the previous week, I showed off a bit, clasping the arm firmly and pushing it upward I removed one arm, and then the other one.

I removed the pyjama jacket. Why didn't dummies have something else on underneath? Feeling very disconcerted to be faced by a nude bosom, I felt my face flush hot, but taking courage, I started to remove the trouser part. But that garment would not budge; Every time I pulled at them they sprung back on their elastic. I felt around the back, more embracing! and found that they were fixed by a pin hammered into the model. Bending down for my pliers I hit my head on the nude upper torso, to a roar of pleasure from the crowd. They must have thought this free entertainment was worth watching, and the boys were constantly shouting advice and rude remarks.

I removed the pin, but nothing was going to make me take those trousers off with that lot watching on the other side of the glass. I grabbed the only dust sheet and threw it over the figure, covering all but the legs and feet. Holding the sheet with one hand to stop it slipping from the shiny figure, I tried to remove the garment with the other, but whichever side I pulled, it only slipped up again.

I figured that if I let the sheet go it would slip off revealing too much, so I ducked underneath the sheet and used both hands on the pyjama bottoms. It was not until I had the garment as far as the knees that I realised that I had set about this job the wrong way; the dummy stood on a heavy stand and the trousers would not come off at all that way.

The noise beyond the plate glass window brought me from under the sheet to look at what was going on out there; I could hardly believe my eyes; the crowd had grown so large that it was now out to the kerb blocking the whole pavement. A policeman had just arrived to see what was going on.

At that very moment there was a shriek of spontaneous laughter from the crowd, and I turned to see that the sheet had slipped off revealing one nude figure with trousers at the knees. The other dummy showed that my efforts to remove the bra were not wholly in vain as half had broken free and it hung seductively down, revealing most of what it was intended to cover.

I threw the pyjama jacket round the shoulders of the bra dummy, and the sheet over the other. As I turned my back the sheet slid to the floor, I walked, red faced to the doorway and as I did the jacket slipped off too. All those people would think I was doing it on purpose. Some might know me, the kids would tell everyone. They would think I was dirty minded. The Police might come for me! I panicked!

Whether the Managing Director was there or not I did not care, I walked out of the window and straight up to the office where I demanded my cards and told them I was leaving their service. The office girls looked in amazement not knowing what had happened or what to do about it. I could not stay and answer questions so I just walked out, I ran all the way home and sobbed my heart out on the bed, listening now and again for the police to come and arrest me. (For what, I was not clear)

No police came, and with great tact the family slowly helped me back to laugh at myself and the whole incident, but I affirmed loudly "I will never go back there again, never!" In the end the situation died slowly and quietly after my Mother visited Walter Cobbs and paid one weeks wages in lieu of notice.

Such was my state of mind, though, it was six or seven weeks before I could accept that the whole district was not talking about me, and that my family, friends and church did not think that I was rude and horrid. It was over a year before I entered the store again as a customer, and even then I was looking for anyone who might remember me as that horrid kid who used to be in the display department! It took even longer before I would go anywhere near a shop or department selling women's clothing.

Chapter 3.

There being nothing suitable in the situations vacant columns of the local paper I caught a tram to Catford to visit the Labour Exchange.

They were rather rude over the fact that I had left my last employer; they did not like it when they learned that I left without giving notice; they liked it still less when I would not explain why I left. As a punishment I was kept waiting all morning and then offered one job, "Take it or leave it, that's all you are going to get today" I was told, so I agreed to an interview with The Wayne Tank and Pump Company in Sydenham.

The position was for Office Junior at fifteen shillings a week, and not far from my home. I was taken on to work in their block of offices. The work was simple and there were three or four others of my own age each doing quite different office junior jobs.

My task was to shuffle papers from one department to another all day long. I was given a large leather pouch with many divisions in it and I made my way through the various offices all over the building putting papers from my folder into the IN trays, and taking papers from the OUT trays to convey to yet more IN trays. It required little more than learning who people were and in which office they were located, and a capacity to keep on walking all day and every day.

Suddenly Winter was over and it turned warm, windows and doors were left open and there were days when one felt that no one ought to be working in stuffy offices anyway. By this time I could work quickly, knew my way about and could sometimes take it a little easy, all work being done. It was on such a day that The Accident Happened!

The firm had what was called "The Record Office," It was a very large room where all the papers ended up in simple single open files. These files were stacked in long rows of steel stack shelves some six feet high and about four or five feet wide standing about three feet apart one behind the other, all crammed with manila folders filled with papers about correspondence, costs, production, customers accounts and such like, all neatly labelled so that the clerks of that department could produce any item on demand.

It was here that I paused to pass the time of day with another office junior, concealed between the first and second stack of shelving. As we chatted we leant our weary bodies against the stack shelf, and before we knew what was happening the shelving was moving under our combined eighteen or twenty stone weight. As it fell away from us there was nothing we could do to stop it, The shelving hit the stack shelves behind it with a crash sending that one toppling and spilling files everywhere: That set of shelves hit the next one with an almighty bang and so on all down the line like a row of dominoes falling.

There were some twenty stack shelves, and the crash of each hitting the other followed by a whoosh of papers was quite frightening.

We beat a hasty retreat through the nearby open 'Fire Exit', to reappear moments later through the bottom door enquiring with a number of others what had happened. We surveyed the scene of devastation, some nineteen file racks had fallen, only one was left standing. The staff of the department were standing in shocked amazement, others had appeared from all over the building to see what all the noise was about and stood with us by the door.

Then the internal phone rang, a girl answered it, she put her hand over the mouth piece and spoke to the supervisor "Mr Richards wants the latest correspondence on Hedges Ltd 304 High Street". The older woman looked at the heap of files and strewn papers "Tell him it's not available" she said. How I admired her quiet controlled voice.

We moved to the first shelving that had fallen and tried to lift it back, "give us a hand" I called to a man by the door, he came and we lifted the stack shelf upright, as we did so more files fell into the heap. We began to pick the files up and place them in the shelves. The supervisor came over "All right boys, I'm sure you mean well but you are making the job of sorting more difficult". She decided on her course of action "Leave everything alone, all of you." there was a real command in her voice "Don't any of you touch a thing". She swept out of the door and headed for the managers office. We removed ourselves from the scene of the crime.

The other lad and I quietened our conscience by reminding ourselves that it was an accident, we would never have done it deliberately. There was no point in saying that WE had done it and maybe getting the sack. As it was no one would be blamed even though it would be a mystery as to how it happened.

In point of fact some good did come from it, for the whole positioning of the shelving was changed, they were afterwards anchored to the wall so that there would be no repeat performance, and some members of staff were paid overtime to get the whole mess sorted out and the department helped back to order.

One evening soon after this, my parents expressed their concern over my future, "There doesn't seem to be any future where you are at the moment, are you interested to make this your life's work?" they asked "Great heavens No!" I exploded "Who could be interested in designing and making petrol pumps or messing about with paper work?" "Then we must pray for some guidance about your future" "You won't always have parents to lean upon you know, you ought to know what you should be doing with your life by now". So I returned to the well worn theme of my future in my nightly prayers.

Two weeks later I received a letter from the firm explaining that due to the depression they had to cut staff, and as I was the last junior to be taken on their staff I must be the first to go. One week later I was again unemployed.

What would happen to me now I wondered?

Once more a two penny tram to Catford brought me to the one place I loathed to visit, The Labour Exchange. There were three queues, one to register as unemployed, this I joined first.

Then there was a second queue to 'sign on'. This was to prove you were not working and once a week could draw, at yet another queue 'your dole' (an unemployment payment given after a certain waiting period, to those who had enough employment stamps on their card).

The third queue was for vacancies. To see what suitable employment was available.

I don't think I was a snob, but I hated mixing with these men who were often dirty, swore continually, and talked mostly about their hoped for sexual conquests or told dirty stories while they waited.

The office staff who ran the system from behind their counters were rude and sharp tongued, treating everyone like a criminal so that you got the impression that to be out of work made you the scum of the earth.

There was always a crowd queuing. From the standing queue you sat on the first place on the wooden benches, and worked your way up, sliding up one place at a time toward the counter. If talking got too loud or someone got up for some reason the clerk would shout at them. There were times when men were punished for answering back or persistent talking, for when they reached the head of the queue they were told to "Go and wait over there 'till you are called". This at the whim of the clerk might be half an hour or an hour. There was nothing that they could do about this if they wanted their dole money at the end of the week or wanted a job. It was commonly accepted that if you upset a clerk suitable jobs would not be offered to you.

When at last you reached the head of the queue you went and stood at the clerk's counter and waited for him to look up at you. If you should speak before this he would slowly and deliberately put his pen down, stare into your face, then shout loudly so that everyone could hear "Are you blind?" the stare would continue "I asked you if you were blind?". "No". Even louder "Then Can't You See, I'm busy?" He would stare a little longer then very slowly and deliberately pick up his pen and continue what every he was doing, keeping you waiting as long as it pleased him.

If you were registering as newly unemployed full details were taken on to a form before you were sent to wait further. If your name was George or Thomas you were alright, but if you were blessed by a fancy name, like Humphrey or similar, it would be repeated loudly for all to hear, and sniggers invited from the assembled crowd. "Oh, you're Algenon are you?" " Algenon? Well you answer to Johnson here". Surnames only were used, it would not be until after the war the 'mister' would be added.

The vacancy clerk would call your surname, and thumb through his cards of possible jobs that he thought might suit you. Here came the tricky bit. If you were not on the dole he could not force you to apply for a job interview, but if you said "no" to several he might tire of you and say that there were no jobs for you. The trick was to offer a cast iron reason why you could not apply for the jobs he offered and that you knew would not suit, so that he could hardly blame you for refusing. "Errand boy wanted at the grocers in the High Street". "I can't ride a bike!" "Well you can learn can't you?". "The shoe-shop want a salesman, ever done that?" "No". "You're not much good at anything are you!" And so it would continue.

When a vacancy was acceptable, the clerk wrote out a 'green card' introducing you to the employer. Armed with this you travelled to the prospective employer for an interview. Sadly the poor employer was often bombarded with applicants with 'green cards', and although he might telephone as soon as he was suited, it often took time to stop the flow.

This left an annoyed employer, and a frustrated applicant who had paid out what little money he had on fares to get there and wasted most of the day. He would then have to return to queue again at the Labour Exchange before he could ask "Are there any other vacancies?.

An interview with a prospective employer was not always easy or enjoyable either. Checking that the backs, as well as the fronts of your shoes were well cleaned, and all clothing was neat and tidy, (for this showed what sort of a person you were and that you cared,) you had to be on time if an appointment was made, which showed that you were a punctual person. But the employer often expected the interview to go all his way, wanting to know everything about you, but saying little about the job, pay, and conditions under which you would work. This is what happened when I went for my next job. Had I have known more I would not have thought it to be suitable.

The job description was Junior Assistant to a Pawnbroker. I was told that I would have to sweep the shop and roll up the steel shutters but was told nothing else, so I thought I would be serving in the shop. Imagine my surprise on my first morning, having swept up I asked for my next task and was taken to a very small door behind the counter which I took to be a cupboard. 'The boss' opened it saying "Follow me". He stepped into the pitch-black cupboard and was gone. I waited for him to put a light on, but he didn't. Then from the darkness came the voice "Come on then".

Leaning forward I stretched out my hands into the darkness, There was a right side wall to the cupboard, a back wall, and some sort of wooden construction on the left. "Come on" compelled the voice again. I stepped gingerly into the cupboard and stood there confused, then I looked up; far away above me there was a dim glimpse of daylight. I thought, it was moving! No it wasn't moving, it was the man somewhere above me silhouetted against some dim daylight far above him.

"Come on", the voice sounded strange in this tunnel, yet more demanding. "How?" I begged. "There is a ladder fixed to the wall, just climb it" was the retort.

I started to climb up in the dark. After the first four steps I stopped and clung there terrified. "I can't" my weak voice wailed. Suddenly the voice above became friendly "All right son, just do what I tell you; hold on to the rung of the ladder and stretch yourself outwards until you feel the wall at your back". I tried, slowly; the wall seemed a long way away, at last I felt it. "Lean your weight on it, you can even take your hands off the rung if you like, you can't fall".

He had more confidence than I did! But I did understand, or feel what he meant. "Now just climb up the ladder feeling your back near the wall". Slowly I climbed. "Don't look down, look up" he counselled. I did, and saw him climb out of the tunnel at the top end. When at last I reached that happy place I discovered another problem, how to put my right leg over a little wooden wall and climb to the safety of the floor? Below me was a sheer drop to several floors. I did it, but with a little help from my friend!

After that I felt worn out and could happily have gone home, but this was to be the beginning of every day that I worked there. I was now on the fifth floor and it was filled with crude wooden racks all holding bundles with numbered tickets on them. We descended via the stairs now unlocking and unbolting each door as we went down. Each room filled with articles which had been pawned.

I learned that poor people who wish to raise money on things which they possessed brought items into the shop below, the man estimated their value and offered them a sum of money that was less than their worth. If they accepted this they 'pawned' the article and were given a pawn ticket as a receipt. If they returned within three months with the ticket they could redeem the article by paying what they had received plus interest. If they did not return to redeem the item within three months it became the property of the pawn broker who sold it to recoup his loss.

My work was to be concerned with the storage and retrieval of the pawned items.

As they were taken in at the counter downstairs they were thrown into a large wicker basket. At the end of each day it was my job to wind a large cranked handle at the top of that same shaft I had climbed, winding the wicker baskets to the top and unloading the pledges, which were mostly bundles of clothing, sheets, and blankets.

During the day I stacked them onto the shelves in number order so that they could be found quickly when needed.

When a customer called to redeem a pledge, the pawn ticket was put into a small cloth bag which hung on a long piece of string running from the shop to the top of the shaft on the fifth floor. This string was attached to a bell fastened onto a coiled spring. When the string was pulled down stairs it rang the bell as a sign that there was a ticket in the bag, I would haul the bag to the top, match the ticket number with the bundle, pin the two tickets together, shout down the shaft "Below!" and throw the bundle down, where it landed with a thud.

After I had been working here for a few weeks I found a way of enlivening the boredom. I discovered that if I was not too prompt in locating the required bundle the little grey head of the 'gaffer' would appear at the bottom of the shaft to enquire "Can't you find it?" or even ask "Are you asleep up there?" So from time to time I would bring a bundle to the top of the shaft and wait. Sooner or later the grey head would appear, and without waiting for his voice I would tip the bundle down, waiting until it had fallen a third of the way before shouting "Below!". The bundle would 'whoomph' on the bottom just missing his disappearing head.

There were many rooms to the building, each was allocated for different kinds of pledges. On the floors below me were rooms full of Crockery, Glassware, cutlery, suitcases, small furniture, musical instruments, clocks, brass work and so on. This was a world I never knew existed before I took the job. Money was so tight for some people that they were always putting something into 'hock', and it kept the man and a woman serving in the shop fairly busy.

Most customers were women and their bundles were mostly of their own clothing, dresses and underwear: The contents would be called out as it was unwrapped, and the garments inspected for holes or wear, "Two shillings" he might say (10p) "can't you make it half a crown?" "No two shillings" "All right then". Some customers were so regular you got to know the faces, some people pawned things to pay the rent or buy food for the kids, others pawned to get money to buy a drink at the pub, or put money on a horse that could not lose, but it usually it did! Some watches, and rings came back to us as if we were their second home. It was not uncommon to be asked to be paid in shillings, and you then knew that the gas meter had run out and there was no money in the house to replenish it, so a visit "To Uncle's" was called for.

All this I gathered from the brief times when I was down in the shop, and from the questions I asked, but most of the time I was upstairs all by myself. This was my kingdom, and it did not take me long to get the hang of the job and deal with it efficiently. I had everything neat, clean and running smoothly in no time.

There were days which would always be slack in the business, very wet days for example when people did not bother to come out. Then I would arrange some diversion for myself. One such was to descend to the clock room, give each of the forty to fifty clocks a few winds and set them going, then I would set each to chime twelve o'clock in two minutes time, and wait for the time when they would go off. It was quite a unique sound as every clock joined in, from Westminster and Winchester chimes, to hour strikers striking in different keys, add in alarm clocks, and cuckoo clocks, and just imagine it! That's right, you can't, but it was fun.

One afternoon I returned from lunch with nothing to do but wait for possible customers, I looked around but could find nothing that needed doing and I felt lonely and bored. Sometimes I could hear the shop sounds drifting up from the shaft, but I could not hear what was being said. To be so far from everyone only heightened my loneliness.

From the junk room I found the legs of an old trestle table and a few bits of chairs, and in no time at all I had made what to me was the inside of a bomber plane to play in. I had been reading some 'Biggles' books, and flying stories, and my mind was full of war planes, so it was no time at all before I was 'flying my bomber,' roaring over enemy territory, with all the noises coming from my mouth, I was just talking to my crew over the intercom when a loud female voice broke in behind me "What DO you think you are doing?". I went cold all over, I had not heard the woman from the shop below come in. I did not know what to do or say. "I should think that you ought to be able to be trusted to get on with your work" she admonished "Stop playing and get all that wood cleared up, and get on with your work". She turned, and departed, not as quietly as she had come!

I put the wood back into the junk room and waited for the boss to come and tell me off, but I waited in vain. I wandered through all the rooms to see what work I could do, I found none. I sat with feelings which changed from 'feeling guilty' for playing during working hours, and 'feeling annoyed' that I should be told to work and not told what I was supposed to do. I was learning a principle of employment I suppose, which seemed to say 'even if you have nothing to do you must always look busy!'.

Two weeks later, following much prayer and discussion with my parents about my future as a possible pawnbroker, it was decided that there was no future for me here and that I should give in my week's notice on Monday and start looking for other work.

Monday morning came and I went to work with a heavy heart, scared of giving notice. Before I could ask to talk with him the boss took me aside "Come over here lad, I want to talk to you". "You know that we're not at all busy at the moment, in fact we are very slack indeed". he paused to make sure I was listening "The fact is that there isn't enough work to employ a junior at the moment, and I'm afraid you will have to leave at the end of the week". I felt great relief " We've been very pleased with your services, and will give you a good reference". he added as if to soften a bitter pill. He looked at me again to see how I had taken it.

At that moment I had a flash of inspiration "There are a lot of firms in this position" I sympathised "It might not be easy to get another job, do you think I could have a little time off during the week to look for work?" He put his arm round my shoulders "Of course you can... let me see.." he stroked his chin "Work today, and then you can come in again next Friday and pick up your full week's pay packet.

In that moment my heart went out to this man, It could not be easy to deal with the poor people and heartbreaking situations he faced every day, having to be firm on one hand and helpful on the other. In this moment I glimpsed a warm heart of kindness and it had it's effect on me. I saw him again on the Friday, we said 'goodbye' and our paths never crossed again.

Back at the church as my voice was coming back as Bass Baritone, I sat with the Bass section and learned to sing from the bottom line of music and harmonize, rather than singing the air. I was not alone, for among the crowd of young people at the church several also now joined the men's section, among them the friend from school, Bernard.

A little gang of us started going out for walks, and some of the girls from the church also joined us. Girls were an unknown, awesome, and almost terrifying species to me, and this closer contact made me aware that they were human beings rather than the untouchable angel type creatures I had thought they must be.

One Sunday, as I was choir librarian, I was putting sheets of music away, when a young choir boy appeared in the doorway and delivered a message that sounded as if he had rehearsed it all the way. "The vicar says, please would you go and see him in his vestry". This was curious, the vicar never sent for people as a rule, and what ever would he want to see me about?

Making my way across the chancel I attempted to knock on the door, not an easy task when the door is a solid six inches thick, and I entered. Addressing the rear end of his bent cassock as he bent to tie his shoe laces I asked "You wanted to see me?" "Ah!" "Well it's not really me that wants to see you" he grunted under the strain of bending double "It's the Sunday School Superintendent, would you be so good as to see him?". "Well, yes," I hesitated "of course". I wanted to ask why and all sorts of questions, but no opportunity was given.

I had never had anything to do with the Sunday School, whatever would the man want to talk to me about? Did he want me to run some message for him? No he had sons to do anything like that. Perhaps he wanted me to go on the treat? No that was months away. Oh No! He must want me to go to Sunday School! I was too old for that, I would tell him so. I rehearsed what I would say to such a request.

I didn't know much about the Sunday School Superintendent, he was a small lovable little man, a bit doddery and he usually mislaid his glasses. He seemed to put them down and forget where he had put them and couldn't see to find them without them.

"Ah" he smiled when I went to him "Wanted to see you. Have you seen the vicar?". I felt tempted to say "Why, have you lost him?" but I just said "Yes". "Oh good, that's a good chap, that's capital!". He removed his glasses to get a better look at me "Well? What do you think of the idea?" He had lost me! "What idea?" he looked bewildered "The idea the vicar talked about, you know. taking a class in Sunday School". "TAKING a class?" it was my turn to look lost, "Surely the vicar told you?". "Me?" I thrust my hands in and out of my pockets nervously "Teach... teach children ... in class?" "Of course dear boy, I thought the vicar had told you".

My mouth was dry "But, I've never taught before in my life. I don't know anything about Sunday School... I've never been to this one.... I don't know what goes on.... I couldn't.. I..." I ran out of steam. "My dear fellow" he put his hand on my shoulder "I thought you knew all about it, the vicar was supposed to have discussed it with you, I'm so sorry!"

He began to search for some paper or book "Where's my glasses?". I picked them up and gave them to him "Well now, we all feel as you do when we start something new, it's really not so difficult... Nothing venture nothing gain!". He ended with a grin.

This all sounded too cut and dried to me and I started to pull out "I'm sorry, but I really wouldn't know what to say to a class". He pulled his glasses off to gaze into my face "The vicar tells me that you have never got less than excellent in Scripture all through your school life. You've won prizes for scripture knowledge, isn't that so?". I felt the net closing in on me "Yes, but I wouldn't know what to say Sunday by Sunday, or where to begin". "Oh, we have a book for that.. A Teacher's Guide.. Where is it", he dithered "Where's those wretched glasses?".

I helped him to his glasses and he thumbed through the Teaching Guide with expertise. He opened the page which I saw bore Sunday's date, he pointed out the Background Material, The Lesson, and the Reading, But I could not take in what he was saying, my heart was making too much noise it seemed.

His glasses removed once more he was talking about other teaching aids, commentaries, books of further information, a concordance, and on and on he went. I only 'came to' at his request for his glasses, and then I was on my way home with a Teaching Guide in my hot little hand, and panic in my cold little heart.

I won't do it! I can't do it! I threw myself on my bed and went through every emotion. Anger, Tears, Determination To Try! Determination Not To Try. To go back and say 'No'. A resolve to think it over. Then I fell to my knees and poured it out to God.

Some time later I got from my knees with a strange peace. I would leave it all in His Hands. If He didn't want me to teach children on Sunday He would stop me somehow. If He did want me to, I would either make a fool of myself or have His help. That was that.

That resolve did not stop me from thinking about next Sunday all through the week. I knew the story well, and I reasoned that there was no point in knowing scripture if you didn't use that knowledge. But secretly I prayed that God would step in and stop me from having to take the class.

Sunday dawned, and I didn't have Chicken pox or anything to else as an excuse, so I went to morning service. Afterward the superintendent approached me, "Thank The Lord" I breathed "He's coming to say I need not go this afternoon". He said nothing of the kind. "Looking forward to seeing you this afternoon". He was so cheerful! "I think you will make a great teacher. Starting today, and still be teaching into your eighties!" he chuckled , and was gone.

The Sunday School met in the church, the boys on one side, the girls on the other with the aisle between them. The youngest children sat in the front pews, and the ages increased as they got further to the back, I hoped that I was not going to teach the teenagers at the back: I wasn't. "This is your class". the super' smiled, introduced me to seven boys who were around seven or eight years old. I took my seat beside them as all the other teachers seemed to do and waited for things to happen.

The first part of the afternoon was conducted from the front by a woman whom I had known vaguely in the church for several years. She was good, and I found myself hoping that I might teach like her someday. But it had to come! The words I did not want to hear "Now go quietly to your classes".

The result was noisy confusion as each child got up, filed out of the pew, and headed for another part of the church. I just stood aside from the stampeding herd and watched where 'my class' should settle. They moved to a pew in the middle of the church sat down and started talking to each other..

I sauntered after them as if I had been doing this for years, and moved into the pew in front, knelt on the seat, leant over the pew back and cleared my throat. Nothing happened! I cleared my throat again more loudly, expecting attention, I didn't get it. They continued to talk, one boy was actually hitting another with his cap to drive home a point.

I waited for them to hush, they didn't, so, taking courage I started "Well then, let's begin shall we?" I introduced my self as their new teacher, and this at least brought the silence of curiosity. "Are you our teacher just for today?" asked one of them "Or our teacher for always?" I wished I knew! My answer was non committal, "I'm not sure, it rather depends. Possibly always". I hoped that this would help my image and their behaviour. "Now, let us get down to the lesson for today". I produced the book and started to read from it. I was soon aware that no one was listening, so I charged in with a question. No one knew the answer. I put the book down and started to tell the story in my own words, with enthusiasm and imagination, and this held their attention. Warming to the theme I started to act some of the parts and this certainly went down well. Then I thought I saw one of the other teacher looking at me waving my arms about so I eased off a bit.

As I was talking I now became aware that there was a sort of game of 'you touch me and I'll touch you' going on, so I concluded the story, and was pleased to have an intelligent question asked. I fell to answering it, but while I was doing so for this one boy I knew that their game was changing to one of 'you clout me and I'll wallop you'. I said "Cut that out", and to my surprise they stopped.

I had finished telling the story, and only five minutes of the allotted twenty minutes had gone, what could I do now? I looked at the teaching guide and was reminded of the background material. I sailed in with it, it took about three minutes. Twelve minutes to go, I thought, whatever can I do next? I started on another bible story, they were not interested, I waffled a bit, and looked at my watch, another ten minutes. Help!

The next ten minutes was like a nightmare. At least once they were hitting each other on the head with hymn books, while I tried talking about their interests, school, homes, nothing seemed to work. At long last I noted that twenty minutes had passed, I looked around, all other classes were still busy, no one moved. "Come on, come on" I said under my breath. They didn't! The other classes were enjoying the lesson, and went on for another SIX and A HALF MINUTES.

The 'Possibly always' teacher became very firmly the 'Just for today' teacher.

I asked for a chat with the superintendent. "How did you get on, dear boy?". I couldn't tell him! But I made my excuses, handed in my teaching guide, found his glasses for him, and left.

Chapter 4.

Have you ever felt as though you were in a sort of 'no mans land'? As if you did not fit in anywhere? It's a very lonely and frightening position. At this time I had left childhood behind and I could never go back to it, but I had no place in the adult world either. I was a misfit!. I could not be a child in Sunday school, nor it seemed could I be a teacher. I was no longer a child at home, but I was just a kid at work. The other young people at the church seemed to know so much more than I did, yet they often acted like children.

The church annual bazaar came, and I wanted to do something to help, but there was no room for me it seemed. "Well" smiled the vicar when I told him "Anything that you can do to raise money will be appreciated". So I looked for a job.

Among the old items in a small ante-room I found an ancient bathchair; it was of wicker construction with two wheels at the back, and one small wheel in front which was connected to a long handle, so that the invalid seated could steer it when, pushed by someone from behind. Swinging the handle around to the front so that I could pull it along, I positioned myself just inside the church hall door on the day of the bazaar, Dressed in fancy costume and with a top hat, I offered my services for a grand guided tour of the bazaar for one penny.

Soon a sporting gentleman took pity on me, paid his penny and sat in the bathchair. I moved off round the hall stopping at each stall and sideshow with comments that every one seemed to find very amusing. I had already worked out witty things to say about the stalls and those who ran them, and at the end of the tour my passenger got out all smiles and said "That was worth sixpence of anybody's money, and gave me the additional coin.

An elderly lady was keen to become my next fare and to my pleasure I found different things to say. This time many people stopped buying from the stalls to watch my progress and hear my patter. One of the younger men of the church entering into the spirit of the thing, took two women's hats from the clothing stall, put one on his head and went around the crowd with the other collecting money.

It was a real triumphant journey right round the hall with everyone laughing and joining in the fun. At last I helped my passenger out of the chair; She stood and looked at me for a moment, then said "It is so good to see one of our young people working so hard for the church, and you enjoyed doing it too, didn't you?". She handed me a ten shilling note "Something else to go in that hat". she smiled.

The two hats now joined me and I was not sure which hat I liked the best. The first was the one that had travelled the crowd, and the contents showed the I had made over two pounds for the church. The other hat was removed from the jolly man who had helped so much, and he proceeded to take me to the tea stall where I enjoyed a nice tea and also discovered a new friend. Perhaps there was a bridge from childhood to manhood after all.

The vicar, giving the notices out one Sunday woke us young folk up by saying "I have a matter I particularly want to talk to the young people about, and I ask them to make a point of being at the youth club this week".

Grouping around after the service we all had suggestions as to what he wanted to say, "The club is going to close down". "No, it is going to open more than one night a week" said another. "More like we've been too noisy or broken something" was another offering. " 'bet he wants us to do something, like keep the church grounds tidy". We just had to wait!

On club night the vicar looked at the good attendance, and started with a question "How many of you know that there is a local Council of Churches?" No one did. "Well all the churches in Sydenham and Forest Hill get together regularly, and we are all very concerned about the youth of the district". "The young people who go to the churches have various church clubs, but others have nothing. We, the churches, are going to do something about that, and we want your help".

As I listened to the plans being unfolded I was completely unaware that what they were talking about was to be the cause of re-routing my entire life. Like a signalman changing the points for a train, it would switch my destination and change my life.

All the churches in the district together were launching a new club for young people. In the main shopping street there was a disused shop with it's living accommodation above, and they had obtained this, and were going to encourage the youth themselves to alter and re-decorate it. It was to be called The ForSyd Youth Centre.

Soon that old shop was a hive of activity. Bricklaying, plastering, woodwork and painting night after night. Youths from different churches worked along side those with no church connection. With dirty hands and a mug of tea, Christians discovered that there were other young people calling themselves Christians, but who went to other churches and had differing ideas about the faith.

Although we viewed each other with real suspicion, and knew that 'Our view was right' and 'theirs was wrong', we all began to realise that we liked each other, and everyone got on well with everyone else.

We mixed cement, knocked down and rebuilt walls, tried to do plastering, and painting...and that painting seemed to go on forever! but during this time we were talking and learning about each other. As for me, I discovered for the first time that there were Methodists, Baptists, Presbyterians, Congregationalists, as well as other Church of England churches, which strangely was a real surprise.

Soon the club was opened, with the main shop part filled with tables and chairs like a cafe. The canteen staffed by our own young people, sold tea, coffee, soft drinks and snacks. And in all my life I have never tasted baked-beans on toast quite like it was then. Upstairs there were rooms for various games and activities, a quiet room, an office and youth leader's room, also a committee room where the young people had a say in the running and activity of the club.

We had a wonderful Youth Leader named Frank who had a magnetic personality. He soon organized outdoor activities as well, and I just couldn't say 'no' when he urged me and others to come and Cheer On our club football team. "I have never seen a football match, I don't know anything about football". I pleaded as I tried to wriggle out of going.

"Come on Gerry" (my new nick name) "Now is the time to learn". So on Saturday I made my way to a football ground for the first time, to enjoy learning about football..

Well wrapped up against the cold I stood behind the white line near 'our goal', while the two teams lined up. A whistle sounded, and all the players started rushing hither and thither after the ball.

I soon lost any idea of which player belonged to which side, but I watched fascinated as the ball was fought for and kicked from one side to the other, with complete disregard for the mud they often fell into or rolled in. All this was done as if there was nothing more important in the world.

The great excitement came whenever the ball came near the goal, and I joined in the cries of "Come on!" "Get it in there" and "Roy, you stupid clot".

As the mass of muddy lads moved away to the other side of the field, I became aware that my feet were freezing cold, I stamped them, and waited for what seemed ages before the action came back. Now I could see some of the lads heading towards us; my! how they could run!

They didn't stop! Before I knew what was happening, the dirty great gritty ball hit me on the side of the face like a sledge hammer, stunning me. It was followed by some hefty player who hit into me like an express train, spinning me round and depositing me in the mud. The whirlwind hurtled straight back into the game without an apology, or asking "are you all right", and when I came to myself neither players or spectators seemed to have noticed that I was sitting in the wet mud, stars leaping around my head in gay abandon.

I got to my feet quickly, in case someone might see me sitting there. I should be so lucky! The spectators were busy leaping up and down shouting like mad, and the players were going mad, some trying to get the ball into the goal and some fighting to keep it out.

I applied one frozen hand to my smarting face, and the other to my overcoat, under which my seat was expressing acute indignation for recent ill use: I was quite unaware that I was adding additional mud to that garment as I rubbed myself, then a shout went up "GOAL!". "Where?". "Whose?". I joined the nearby group and discovered that 'We had a goal'. The players were happy and showing much love for each other, which was nice.

I was very happy for them, so we had won, great, and now we could go home, I was frozen, except for the left side of my face which seemed on fire. I waited for the supporters to move away. They didn't. "Oh No! They were starting to play all over again". They kicked the ball about at the far end of the field, and there it seemed to stay most of the time. Twice there was a 'Goal!' but the group around me seemed to have lost the delight they once had in such things.

At long long last, just as I was wondering if I had any legs at all, they were so cold, the game came to a merciful end, and I prepared to leave. Then Frank arrived, thrust a plate of sliced oranges in my hand saying "You take this one, and you take this one". to others. How nice!. "Mind you don't drop them as you go" Then I discovered that these were to be taken out to the players. It was quite a shock to discover that this was only the interval.

It was good to walk, even if it was through mud most of the way. but the conversation was all centred on the game, did I see this, and did I see that happen? You would think it was an international disaster that we were losing two / one. What did it matter I wondered, it was only a game!

Soon the game was restarted, I could not understand things like 'Offside', 'Corner kick', or why the little whistle went several times to stop the game. I did know that I was so cold I could not remember being so cold as this before, and I longed and prayed for the game to end. My prayers were greatly delayed before being answered!

I went home to be told off by Mum for getting mud all over my clothes, I awoke Sunday morning with a cold, it turned to influenza, and I was in bed for over a week. "Bloomin Football!" I said bitterly "It will be a long time before I ever go again". and I have never seen football played since. Later, when I discovered that people made money out of football, gambled on it with pools, and paid players vast sums of money to play, I grew to have a hatred of the game. And now that thugs use the game for fighting and rioting I am thankful that I can happily live without it.

I respect those who like football, they must feel upset at my experience, but gentlemen, it IS only a game, and you will insist on playing it when it is so cold and wet!

I enjoyed sitting in the club canteen each night with a group of young people from other churches. I just couldn't understand it, they didn't accept that The Church of England was THE church, right and perfect in every way, and I found it tough going to defend it.

The Methodists seemed to think we should accept the teachings of Wesley and change our ways. The Baptists said our christening of infants was not biblical, and that Confirmation was a man made system to cover up for our errors in baptism. The Congregationalists said our church government was unscriptural and Roman Catholic in form. Only the Presbyterian said little. One word that did come up time after time was 'Converted', and I was not at all sure what they were talking about.

I would hasten home to scour my bible for the answers, only to return to more questions about the Prayer Book, or why our clergy were dressed in robes, or what was the biblical reason for having an altar. I called on my vicar with a long list of questions, but although he seemed to have the answers I didn't seem to understand what he was talking about.

I also asked him to help me as to what God wanted me to do with my life. He talked about talents and the gifts God has given us, told me to pray about it and look for the answers that God would give.

So I prayed, and looked. There in a Christian newspaper was an advert inviting young Christians who were in the Church of England to join The Church Army. So I wrote an application for an interview.

The Church Army was the C of E version of The Salvation Army. It had been started, I discovered, by Wilson Carlisle, who went onto the streets preaching The Gospel, armed with a trombone. I was invited to the London headquarters to see a certain Captain, so off I went. The interview took place in a large top floor office room. There were desks everywhere with men and women in grey uniforms, and typists, office workers and busy people moving about everywhere. I sat opposite the elderly Captain trying to answer the many questions he put to me, in spite of telephone bells and distraction all around.

Suddenly a loud bell rang. "I shall have to leave you for about ten or fifteen minutes" the Captain said "You don't mind waiting?". "Of course not". what else could I say? He got up from the desk and left. So did everyone else! Talking to each other they drifted to the door like water moving toward a sink plug hole. Soon they were all gone, the sound of their conversations slowly disappearing, a door closing somewhere, and all was strangely quiet.

"Funny people!" I thought. Not a soul left in the office, they've ALL GONE! "Gosh!" I said to my self, "I know what it is, that was a Fire Bell and they have gone on a practice fire drill." "They might have taken me with them. Suppose it is not just a practice? Perhaps the building is on fire, Help!". All remained peaceful. I spent some time trying to work out what had made them all leave like that. No solution came. I looked at my watch, ten minutes gone, I looked again and again, fifteen minutes. Not a sound from anywhere.

Then after some twenty minutes, the sound of feet, and more feet, they were coming back. In they burst, each returning to whatever they were doing as if nothing had happened. My Captain came and sat down. "What happened?" I asked "Oh" he said as if everyone else in London knew the answer "That was our morning prayer time".

Following that interview I accepted an invitation to attend a Training Weekend at their Centre in Maiden Early. With other possible recruits I learned about their work of evangelism in the churches, filled in forms, had interviews, discussion groups and talks. Several times I was asked "Are you

Saved?" I said I didn't know quite what that meant, "but I most certainly love God and want to serve Him."

I was deeply impressed by the love everyone had for God and other people; and the devotions held in the chapel were thrilling, I could never remember feeling so close to God. The effect was to last for weeks after. From the Church Army's point of view the weekend was to show if we were suitable recruits, I wasn't it seemed, so there the matter ended. Another door had closed.

I came away with a desire to find out what it meant to be 'Saved' or 'Born again'. I asked various people at the church, they didn't know it seemed. I think I must have asked the vicar at a busy time for he didn't get around to telling me, others seemed embarrassed as if it was not a subject to be talked about. I just couldn't find out. I certainly was not going to ask the young people from other churches at the club, so when talking with them I just pretended I knew all about it.

The Forsyd Youth Centre used the Baptist church hall monthly for it's Parliament. This was the democratic method of it's government. Seats for club members were arranged each side, as in The House of Commons, We had a Speaker who entered the House, preceded by a Mace Bearer to start the sessions, and all business before the house was addressed through 'Mr Speaker'. The Youth Leader was The Prime Minister, The Government were those who had been elected to hold some office in the club. I recall that the House was most unruly when the club football team lost, as it usually did, and more than once the Minister for Football was call on to "resign". It taught us quite a lot about democracy and I believe that our parliament was much more orderly and pleasant than the one in Westminster, which I have always thought was like a lot of school kids squabbling.

The Methodist hall was used for keep fit and dancing events. The Holy Trinity hall was used for dramatics, as it had a good stage, and The Congregational hall was used for social and educational gatherings that would not fit into the club premises. This meant that we got used to the various church halls in the district, but we did not see each others churches.

From my many conversations with those from other churches it seemed to me that there were many differences, and I was ignorant of what they all did and believed. So I resolved to visit every kind of church denomination for a Sunday act of worship, to see what they were like and also to try to find out how they interpreted the Christian Faith.

I wrote out a list of the different churches, and decided to start with one with which I had no connection or knowledge at all. I chose The Quakers, or Society of Friends, who advertised their services outside a large house which I had passed, often wondering who or what they were.

With feelings of guilt over walking past my own church I made my way to The Quaker Hall of Meeting whose service was advertised for 11am. I arrived soon after 10-30 am. Early as always! They had just opened the door. The room I entered was a large square room of a house, it had a small table in the centre, with two rows of chairs arranged all round it in a circle. I sat on one near to the door for ease of escape, and waited for the service to start.

About ten or twelve people came, they smiled at me and said "Good Morning" as they entered, and sat somewhere in the circle in silence. I peeped at my watch, it was two minutes past eleven, "They are LATE in starting" I thought. I waited, then looked at my watch, eleven minutes past, "They ARE late in starting". At 11-20 I mentally apologised to them, "They must start at 11-30".

I sat in the silence deciding to pray by my self until they started their service. I gently peered at my watch again, 11.29 am "Oh good, they'll start at 11.30 I expect". That didn't! I started again to recite all the prayers that I could remember from the C of E Prayer Book. One more look showed 11-39 am "Oh for goodness sake SAY SOMETHING, SOMEBODY!" I felt despair. "Suppose they went on like this for hours? What should I do?".

By 11-40 am. I had gone through every prayer I could remember, and prayed for everyone I could think of. I turned to wonder what would happen if in this silence I suddenly shouted out real loud "Hallelujah!". I smiled as I pictured the old lady opposite jumping out of her skin, and the fat man in the corner, who looked asleep, jumping up, his glasses falling off the end of his nose. The staid couple over there would probably say "Really!" in disgusted tone.

I smiled at my thoughts. All through my childhood my Father had often said "I'll show you a penny if you sit perfectly still and quiet for one whole minute". Boy! he should see me now. At the end of the minute he always took a penny from his pocket and showed it to me, then put it back; but I always got the penny in the end. I could make a fair bit of money if he were here in this place I thought. I had been still and silent for well over an hour, what could I think about now?

I decided to picture some of the stories of Jesus, to see in my mind the crowds following Him, 'See' Him healing people, feeding the five thousand. My mind was lost for a while in such story land pictures. I looked at my watch, it was nearly twelve. I felt more peaceful than I could remember before and the last ten minutes had been great. Suddenly someone moved, after such quietness the sound was like a deafening whirlwind as a man got to his feet. He gave a few notices of coming events, read a verse of scripture, and everyone smiled in relief, got up, and went home. As we sat at lunch Mum said "Did you have a good service?", I smiled "Those Quakers are a funny lot, I don't think that they'll tell me much about what they believe". I commented. So with that, another door closed.

"If only I had taken the trouble to find out about The Quaker Meeting before I went, it would have been better" I explained to the family. "I'm going to find out about Methodism before I go this week, I have an appointment with their Minister". "Is that where you'll go next Sunday?" "Yes".

My first impression about the Methodist Minister's house was that it was extremely old fashioned and tatty, The furniture was very old and in poor condition, worse than I had seen in second hand shops. Was this part of their belief? Were they called to live like St Francis, in poverty?

The Minister himself seemed well educated, and there was a picture on the wall of his fellow students in college days. I asked questions about his church and their beliefs. His replies were confusing as he spoke about Circuits, which made me think about electrical wiring, Society Stewards,

Superintendents, and Conference. He spoke as if everyone knew about such things so I did not want to show my ignorance to ask further.

I asked him what was meant by being saved and got the impression that Methodism was in some way divided about this, and before I knew it we were onto the subject of temperance. "You will find that there is little difference between us and the Church of England" he affirmed "after all Methodism came out from there". So I promised to visit his church on Sunday.

It was different. They did not process in, had no altar, used a different hymn book with none of the hymns I knew, and used a different Prayer Book. They did have a most amusing choir mistress who conducted the choir with elbows sticking out and flapping like a chicken, she looked so funny from the rear view that I laughed into my handkerchief until the tears rolled down my cheeks as she conducted the anthem. Some young people were in attendance who I knew, and some more that I did not know, but with which I enjoyed good company after the service was over.

Perhaps the biggest shock was sitting for prayers instead of kneeling. Also having to look to what everyone else was doing being unsure what to do next. On the whole I liked it but got the impression that, like my own church their Christianity was very much 'the done and accepted thing'. It was different but not the fresh, or real sincere worship of God I thought I was looking for.

Frank, our youth leader, was a Deacon at the Baptist Church. I had tried to picture him on Sundays dressed in long flowing robes serving at the altar. "This I must see" I said to Mum, so off to the Baptist Church I went.

Sydenham Baptist Church was in the main road of shops and had a formidable entrance at the top of a vast flight of steps. I could not imagine what lay behind those big brown open doors, all I could see was a partition with notices on it. I stood looking in the window of the large china and glass shop near by, through the reflection of the glass window I could watch the people going in to church. I waited until at least half a dozen had gone up those steps before I took courage to follow.

Across the road, up those steps, in through those doors, and I had made it. I was greeted with a smile, a warm handshake, and a hymn book. (What no prayer book?) Inside, the church was plain, but neat and tidy. No altar, but the centre had a raised pulpit with a Communion Table in front of it; As I had found in the Methodist. Either side of the Table but set some distance away, were two rows of chairs which I later found to be for the choir who did not have robes as ours did.

I sat for a prayer, noticing that there were no hassocks, so this was going to be another church where they sat to pray. Then there was a swish of curtains at the front, and someone was descending the few steps from the premises beyond, it was Frank! He saw me at once and hastened to me (without bowing to the communion table as he passed, I noted) "Gerry" he smiled "How nice of you to visit us".

"I hope you are not playing hooky from your own church?" he looked concerned, so I explained my desire to find out about other churches. He seemed relieved. Dropping my hand from a long warm handshake he said "Come and meet some of the people". I moved out of the pew and followed him. "This is Gerald Gossage, Gerry to his friends" he introduced, and to all those who had so far arrived I enjoyed a warm and friendly welcome. In the way he spoke I felt that he was proud of me, and this made me happy; within a few minutes I knew something of all those present. "Let me show you around" Frank offered, and there followed a tour of the buildings. As we headed back toward the church he asked "Aren't you in the choir at your church?" "Well, why not sit in the choir this morning with me".

I enjoyed the worship that morning, even if they did not kneel for prayers, the freshness, warmth and sincerity of those prayers were a new experience in talking with God. The singing was loud, hearty and taken at a faster pace than I had previously known, and I had a good time singing. Most of all I liked the sermon, it helped and inspired me and I came back to it's theme again and again during the following week.

I learnt that their Minister was just leaving their church after being with them for many years, so I decided to ask Frank some of the things I wanted to know about Baptists.

I discovered that they looked to the New Testament for ordering their church. They were quite independent of any authority outside their own local church, and ran the church by the prayerful discussions and decisions of the Members of The Church made at a monthly Church Meeting.

Deacons were men and women elected by the church for their Godliness; and that they carried out the decisions made by the Church Meeting. The Baptists did not christen babies, but dedicated them, without the use of water: but adults were Baptised in a large baptistery pool which was under the platform now holding the communion table.

People came into membership of the Baptist church on publicly professing that Jesus Christ was The Lord of their life, and was their Saviour, following an interview with the Minister and acceptance by The Church Meeting.

Frank finished his explanations with "It's all in the New Testament, this is how God ordered it, this is what we try to follow".

It left me with a lot to think about, and I found out a load more from two books Frank loaned me when we met during the week.

My following Sunday morning at the Congregational Church seemed almost a repeat of that at the Baptist Church. The warm welcome, form of worship, and preaching, this time by a Welsh man, had the same effect on me. "What is the difference?" I asked their Minister "Bless you, Bach! not much difference at all". he boomed "The only difference is one of baptism, like your own church we baptise children, as well as adults, they only baptise grown ups". I borrowed some books on Congregationalism and found out that both churches came out of the Reformation, with the desire to get back to the Bible teaching and authority in all things.

There was no Salvation Army where I lived but I was keen to find out what it was like to sing to a band instead of an organ, and know what they did, so I journeyed to The Salvation Army Citadel in Catford. It turned out to be a small hall with a well scrubbed wooden floor and rough benches. As a young person I summed it up as 'very poor and old fashioned'. The greeting was very warm, and I was called 'brother'. There was no altar or communion table here, but a form facing us and the band behind it.

The music was even faster, and very loud, I wondered what the neighbouring houses thought of all this disturbing of Sunday peace. The prayers were addressed to God as if He were a great pal of theirs who eagerly waited to do their bidding, and God was reminded several times with the expression "You know, Lord..." But it was sincere, and it was better than reciting the same prayers week after week I thought.

The sermon contained much repetition and a good mixture of theological words with the common language. The message was that we were all sinners and we needed to "Come to the mercy seat". Whatever that was I was not sure.

There followed a rousing hymn, and a prayer that went on and on. "Oh Lord Thou knowest that there is one sinner here this morning who needs to come to the penitent form". After a while I got the idea that they were meaning me, and that their service would never end until I did what they wanted me to do, I didn't know just what that was, and as we were all praying I could hardly ask anyone. I thought of my Mother who would soon have dinner on the table, and I still had a journey to make home, I waited, and waited, but their prayer continued, so I quietly slipped out and made for home.

Years later I was to learn what wonderful people they were in The Army, and I was to come to love them, but just at this stage in my development I crossed them off my list as a funny lot with whom I wanted to have no truck at all.

Now that I had visited the other churches I resolved to settle down to be a good Anglican, I threw myself into the work of the church, enjoyed singing in concerts as well as in church, and was determined to put from my mind all that I had experienced in other churches. But Sunday by Sunday I became more frustrated with the services. I just could not be sincere toward God while going through the same old order of worship and prayers. I was restless and unhappy. All my prayers for help seemed to go unanswered.

I went to see the vicar to seek his help. He seemed to think I was anti-church. I explained "The last time that you said The Lord's Prayer did you think of everything you were saying and mean it?" He laughed this off saying "But you WERE saying your prayers, that is all that matters". I did not think that God wanted to hear me recite prayers, but how can you tell a vicar that? I am sure he tried to be helpful but he wasn't.

Just after this our dear old organist and choirmaster, Mr Larkman died. After his funeral the church didn't seem the same anymore. I prayed and thought for a whole week, then sat down and wrote a letter resigning from the church and all the offices I held. I laid it before my little cross and prayed that God would stop me from sending it if He didn't wish it to go. There seemed no answer.

Slowly I arose from my knees, walked to the vicarage, slowly opened the letter box and let the letter slip through. I felt a pain of panic and sorrow as I walked back home. I had cut the cord that bound me to the church, my childhood, and whole past life. I felt lonely and scared. I wished that I hadn't done it, yet knew that I had to. I reached the gate of our house, turned to look at the church I knew so well as it stood opposite, turned my back on it and went up the path with tears on my cheek. What would happen to my life now?

Chapter 5.

The days that followed were gloomy indeed. I no longer belonged to The Church. My upbringing had instilled into me that 'The Church' was The Church of England, and I had resigned from it. Even if I recognised that The Church was also these other denominations I still did not have a church allegiance. But the larger gloom that gripped me was a little voice inside which kept suggesting that now I had left the church I need never go back. "You can be just as good a Christian outside the church" it suggested. "You have only seen life from inside Christian circles, now is the time to do other things with your time". The voice nagged at me day by day. Finally it suggested that I take just one Sunday off, "Surely that can't hurt?" So I did.

I was just learning to ride a bicycle and I had got Father's permission to do something to the shed so that I could ride straight up the path and into the shed. (like a car driving in) So on Sunday I started, and while people were going into my old church opposite, I was hammering in nails. I told myself "I don't care if you do all look, I just don't care!". But deep down I did care, and I felt dreadful about treating the Lord's

Day as if it were no different from any other, hammering, and sawing as if it were a weekday.

The day was full of tension and upset somehow and I felt bitterly unhappy. I kept thinking of a day when I had rebelled once before. I had been about twelve years old at the time. I recalled that there had been a film on at the local cinema which the boys at school had said they were going to see. I had said that I would be in church not going to the pictures, they had called me stupid, a sissy and all kinds of other things.

When it had been time to get ready for church I had revolted. "Why can't I go to the pictures like other boys" I had asked, expecting Mother's anger. She looked at me, now I was in trouble I thought. Then she just said "All right if you want to go to the pictures, I'll go with you". Was I hearing right? Mum saw my appearance. "Take that Eton Collar off, that's what you wear in the choir, and change into your every day suit". ... "Hurry up now!" I rushed upstairs to change, amazed at my Mother's attitude. When I came down she had changed also and was ready in the hall. My Father and Brother were getting ready for church, I was going to the pictures; I was not too sure how to deal with this. I felt a mixture of satisfaction and confusion.

Outside the cinema there was a queue for the cheaper seats, we joined it. "Mum, can we pay the extra and go straight in?" "Why?" "Well someone from the church might see me going to the pictures". She neither looked at me or showed any expression on her face "If you say that there's nothing wrong in going to the cinema on Sunday then you mustn't be ashamed to be seen doing what you say is right". "Oh please Mum, you can take it out of my pocket money". I had pleaded "Several weeks pocket money I should think". she murmured "for you will be paying for your own seat tonight". "All right, But, Please Mum!". We had slipped out of the queue and straight in for the dearer seats, up in the balcony.

I started to watch the screen, but I could not concentrate for long. My eyes kept wandering to the cinema clock on the wall. "Reg and Dad would be leaving for church in a few minutes". Some adverts came on. Then the spotlight shone upon the sales girls selling sweets and ices and the lights went up. I slid down in my seat in case someone should see me, "fancy them selling ices, things like that ON A SUNDAY!" I thought. I knew that my Mother would not offer me an ice on Sunday, but she always had when we went to the pictures before.

How pleased I had felt when the lights lowered and the big picture started. I saw the clock illuminated in the darkness. They would all be going to church now. I could just make it if I went now. The clock moved so slowly, I could still get to church.

"Mum" I whispered "I think I'd rather go to church". No response! "Mum" a little louder "I think I'd rather go to church". "Quiet dear, watch the film". The clock had hardly moved. "Mum, I'm going to go to church". She bent over me and whispered "I've paid good money for these seats now and you are going to watch the film". The clock had moved on, if I didn't go soon I'd be late. "I want to go to church Mum". Someone behind shushed at me. I pictured my brother going into the vestry. I made up my mind. "Mum". "Mum" "I want to go to church". "Well for goodness sake go" said a voice nearby. I got up and pushed past the people and rushed out. I ran all the way home. Up to the bedroom, changed into my

Sunday suit, put on my collar, and I was off, and ran all the way!.

I had arrived at the church just as the vicar entered for a prayer in the vestry. "Come along lad get your cassock and surplice on, hurry". I did, and processed in with red face and still out of breath. During the first hymn I saw Mum slip into the pew next to Dad. I said a little prayer of 'thanks'. I had come back home!

So now, on this second occasion of Sunday revolt I managed to get as far as tea time feeling just as miserable as I had been before when I had tried the pictures instead of church. I could find no happiness this way. Now I knew in my heart what I had to do. As soon as tea was over, I went to my room, knelt down and repeated the prayer of General Confession. When I came to the words "We have followed too much the devices and desires of our own hearts" it went right home to my heart. With tear-filled eyes I stopped there and just said "Sorry Lord". Within moments I was washing my tear stained face, putting on my Sunday suit, and heading for Sydenham Baptist Church.

I returned home at ten o'clock that night singing a new hymn I had learnt, for after a great service I had spent the evening with their young people and I felt great. I had experienced such a happy evening. After this I went there every Sunday, was soon accepted as a full choir member, and felt that I was back home!

With my membership of The Forsyd Youth Club came also the opportunity to join the Dramatic section. In my school days I had always enjoyed taking part in the school plays, but had never been entrusted with a speaking part.

I had always been shy and self-conscious in the company of others, except when I was discussing Christianity around a table, now I found I had a previously hidden talent, I could act! When I took on a part I just became that person and all trace of ME disappeared.

I was most encouraged by the first play I took part in; I took the part of a reporter sent to get a story about a haunted house. In the closing curtain I had to die of shock at seeing this ghost. I so lived the part that I tingled all over as I was supposed to see this ghost and 'died' so realistically that there was an audible gasp from the audience, and when it was all over several people said nice things about my portrayal of the part.

Tim Say our producer was a wonderful man, he knew just what he wanted from us and just how to get it. I learned so much about acting from him.

We put on more and more plays for charity, and now the war effort, and as I was given more important parts one problem began to loom large, my appearance was spoiled by my teeth!

I had never been to a dentist because of my condition of bleeding and now my teeth were very bad, and it showed! I visited a dentist who told me there was little worth saving but that he would not risk extracting any of them without my own doctor being present. I guess you couldn't blame him. So I got on to my doctor and he agreed to let me have one tooth out while he was there. This started a tooth pulling process!

The rules they made were.. only one tooth extraction at a time, and then only after the previous one was well on the way to being healed.

This meant that after each tooth extraction I would have to wait for three or four weeks before the appointment for the next one out. Sometimes I would get all keyed up ready for the next one, only to be told "No I think we will leave it another week before we do the next." I began to hate those visits more and more. Sometimes the extractions would be with gas, other times local injections. I still remember with horror those visits: It was especially a problem when the front four teeth finally came out, and I found it difficult to talk.

Just as these four front teeth were removed the club decided to take part in a major youth drama competition. We were to present a short five-minute play plus a scene from Macbeth. I was to take the part of Macbeth! I pleaded my situation with the dentist, and as he could hardly put my teeth back he agreed to make me a temporary denture which would have four front teeth for me to display. Within a week or two I was walking around with the best front teeth I had ever known, and I could talk without a lisp!

The rehearsals went ahead and we had high hopes of winning the cup and money prize for the club which the competition offered. However all was not quite so well with the teeth. As the gums shrank over the weeks, the denture began to rock about and was uncomfortable.

Finally the night of the competition arrived, our club was the last of the youth clubs to perform and this did nothing to quell the butterflies in our stomachs. Then I was 'on' and I threw myself into the part of Macbeth. All went well, until we came to the part where Macbeth realizes that Burnam Wood is moving toward him and that it is the enemy camouflaged with trees. I started the lines "Arm! arm! and out...there is no flying hence nor tarrying here" On the word "flying" my four tooth denture came flying out of my mouth and rattled across the stage, I knew I could not continue without teeth, so without a pause I strode dramatically across the stage, bent down, picked them up, held them aloft in dramatic gesture, thrust then in my mouth, and carried on "Ring the alarm bell ..!"

The cast were laughing uncontrollably and I began to be aware by the noise level that humour had invaded this serious play. I looked to the audience of which I could only see the first two rows through the glare of the footlights; those I could see were in various bent positions, some with handkerchiefs held to their eyes, one women was holding her sides and shaking with laughter, an elderly man was laying back with mouth open and tears streaming down his face making funny little gasping noises.

The scene ended thankfully with the curtains closing to drum beats as the troops were supposed to be amassing, but the laughter in the hall grew as the story of my teeth was repeated to those further back, and this finally concluded with clapping which reached great applause and whistles.

We did not win the competition! But in the summing up one of the judges said "Some of us wish there was a prize tonight for the most humorous performance!... Macbeth" he said "will never be the same again, will it!"

I rather thought that my fellow youth club members would be annoyed with me for spoiling their chances of winning the cup, but instead I seemed to become quite popular, even if I was teased unmercifully.

The next bit of fun came when we produced a play called "She Passed Through Lorraine" which was about Joan of Arc. I was given the part of Father Michael and during the play I had to carry around a dead chicken. This presented a problem for you could not just go out and buy a chicken during those war days. We made a chicken with the aid of an old stocking (also difficult to come by) but while it could be used for rehearsals, it looked nothing like a real dead chicken.

The solution came when the father of one of the cast promised us the loan of a real dead chicken for the performances, but we did not appreciate that the play was to be performed on Wednesday the 10th, Thursday 11th and Saturday 13th May, and the bird would be killed on a farm many miles away and be transported, which was a long time to keep a chicken in those days before deep-freezers. It was decided to keep it in someone's fridge' as much as possible and hope for the best.

All went well for the first two performances, and on the Saturday the lad's father brought me the chicken saying that after the final curtain, I was to auction it to the highest bidder to help the charity for which we were performing.

It was a warm May evening and the hall was packed with people, added to this the stage lighting greatly increased the temperature on stage. I noticed that the bird did not smell too nice when it was given to me, but as the play got under way I realised that I was tending to hold it at arms length and that the other actors and actresses were keeping well away from the smell.

After the interval the smell was getting beyond a joke and the front rows of the audience were getting uneasy about it too. It didn't help the cast to keep straight faces when one old lady in the front row took out a pretty little lace hankie and held it to her nose for the rest of the performance.

The play ended and we took our curtain calls. I walked forward and with as much sincerity as I could muster I thanked the anonymous donor of the chicken, saying that he had generously offered it to be auctioned on behalf of the charity. I called for bids, there were none! Then one the cast offered "a penny to take it away" and I felt embarrassment flowing over me, what could I do?

Finally the lad's father came to my rescue by offering 'ten shillings' (50p) (more than it's worth!) someone at the back who was perhaps too far away to smell it, called eleven shillings, and in the end the father got it for twelve shillings and six pence.

For sometime after this my 'friends' pretended to avoid me, with comments about something they could smell, and when discussing the next production some wag made a formal proposal that "before purchasing any new scripts a search be made through them to ensure that no dead birds were required to be used in the play".

I must say that I enjoyed the stage so much, whether comedy, variety, drama, or singing, and I began to wonder if this was where I would make my living. I began to think it more so when, being off sick with 'flu, the producer sent me a letter in which he said "You have the rare talent of putting yourself into the part of the character you are portraying. "For the first time my desire to become a Minister in the Church had a serious rival, especially as The Ministry seemed an impossible goal.

While I was wondering if the stage was my road for the future, a very small thing convinced me it was not. A group of us were reading through plays for possible future production when one lad looked up from the script he was reading with "this is it, this is good!" I looked through the play he was so keen on and was shocked! "You can't put this on!" I said "One of the characters is drunk most of the time and uses foul language all the way through it"

The thought came to me even as I said it, if I were a professional actor I would not always be in productions that were fun, clean, and contained good moral standards. I would probably either have to be a good out-of-work actor, or have to compromise my moral standards.

I recalled to mind my many early visits to the Penge Empire and Lewisham Hippodrome, I remembered some of the unpleasant entertainers I had seen, their lewd jokes, and language with double meanings. No, I was not at all sure I was going to be on the stage. Plays were stories about real people and many of them were bad characters who were dramatised 'warts and all'. To put myself in their shoes, to be like them, even for a little while would not be much fun I thought.

I now see that it was easy for me to put my self in other people's shoes, I often copied others, and it caused a lot of fun and sometimes got me into mischief. I suddenly realised one day that I was talking in the exact tone of voice as someone who had just left me. It dawned on me that I was always mimicking the voices of those around me, usually unaware that I was doing it. I became very embarrassed when I found myself talking in an American southern drawl to a friend because I had just left the cinema, and the mood of the film was still with me. And on another occasion I found myself speaking to the family in 'braid Scots' having just listened to that accent on the radio.

I started to play practical jokes with copied accents after an incident one day. It happened that I had a friend who had a Scottish accent, and while talking to him I agreed to phone up a pal of ours to see if he would go out on a trip with us.

Entering the phone box while Jock waited outside I started to explain what we planned to do. "Is Gerry coming?" he asked "This is Gerry talking" I said "Come off it Jock" came the reply "with your accent I'd know you anywhere". I turned it into a joke, but it was the beginning of many leg-pulls.

There was one memorable evening when, being with two others I accepted a dare to phone one of the church Deacons. The three of us crowded into the phone box, and when the good man answered, I put on a broad Irish accent, and was asking why 'The Father' could not hear "me' confessions".

The Deacon was most patient explaining that it was a Baptist Church not Roman Catholic, they had a Minister not a Father. I caught on the word Baptist as he used it again, and replied that "I was baptised, when I was a little fella'. By Father O'Connor so it was."

The only problem I had was the giggling from the other two in the box; but I held a ten minute conversation with the good man without his suspecting. Well if he did suspect he never let on, and vanity still persuades me that I got away with it: And what it did to my ego image among my friends was nobody's business.

On the other hand it did nearly get me a black eye from a chap only bit older but a lot bigger than me, one night. He thought I was taking the mickey out of the way he spoke. I only just managed to talk my way out of it!

I must have been a shocker for I was always playing tricks with other people. When walking with another friend through a busy London street we would suddenly stop and look up toward the top of one of the big buildings, we would point, and make comments until we had quite a few people standing gazing with us. I would signal to him with a touch on his foot so that we both gasped together, followed by "I thought he'd fallen!" We would move about to get a better view, then quietly move off, leaving a crowd trying to find out what they were supposed to be looking at.

Another dodge I did from time to time was on the London Underground. I would stand near the tunnel entrance and look into the tunnel while doing some quite realistic bird calls. People would gather around to look for the bird, and occasionally someone would even say that they saw it, or heard its wings as it flew further into the tunnel. You can imagine how it made my day on one occasion to hear three women making comments like "Poor thing" and "What will it do when the train comes through the tunnel?" "It'll get killed I should think", "No, it's got enough sense to get out of the way I should hope".

My Mother and I both had a keen sense of humour, and there were times when we would laugh until the tears streamed down our faces and we got a pain in our sides.

Like the evening she and I boarded a number 108 bus with my brother. These particular buses had long cushioned seats running length wise on the lower deck, and as mother and I sat on the near side long seat, Reg took the seat opposite us. Reg has always been a big heavy fellow and he chose to sit right to one end of the cushion. Seated on the other end of my brother's seat was a quite small woman, her feet not touching the floor. As Reg dropped his full weight on his end of the cushion it acted rather like a see-saw. The little woman was catapulted into the air some six inches up, coming down with a plop!

The look she gave Reg was as black as thunder, but he was quite unaware of what he had done. The conductor came for the fare, Reg rose to his feet to reach his trousers pocket saying "I'll get them". "No!" called Mum, fearful of the little woman's plight, but a little late. Reg sat down again. The woman was again shot into the air, nearly falling from her seat as she landed.

Mother and I were now trying not to laugh for fear of offending the woman, and so concerned over the situation that the fare was not coming forth very quickly. Reg once again decided to pay, standing to reach his pocket. The little woman reached out for a hand rail a little too far away for comfort, and clutched it for dear life. Seeing what was coming her way she dropped her feet to the floor and adopted a half standing bent posture. She was in this position when Reg dropped his full weight on the other end giving the woman a resounding slap on the bottom.

Whether she had reached her destination at this point or not we will never know, but she pressed the bell for the bus to stop, gave us all a very black look, and got off the bus. The innocent look on my brother's face who had no idea what he had done, plus the pent up laughter gave way to so much mirth that it was a long time before we could tell Reg what we were laughing about.

My Father was a more serious man and humour came to him more slowly. Like the time when he entered the house very upset about something. He was standing there still in his hat and coat telling mother in a very irate voice about what ever had gone wrong, and we two boys were watching his anger. Suddenly to express his feeling he took off his hat with a sweep and threw it onto the floor and stamped his foot on it. His flow stopped as he saw that we were all looking down at his hat. There was silence for a brief moment, slowly a smile came on to all our faces as we viewed the poor hat, and I said in a very quiet voice "Is it dead Dad?"

To watch his face change from anger to a smile that grew larger and blossomed into a full laugh was fascinating to watch, and the incident became a family joke for some time to come.

One of the family laughs came about too over Dad's new shed. It started by Dad announcing to Mother that he was going to build a new shed in the garden. Now poor old Pop (as we called him) had never had a woodwork lesson in his life. He was essentially a Hammer and Nails man and his screwdriver was used more for taking lids off paint tins than turning screws, so as a youngster I was most intrigued as to how he would go about a new shed.

No plans were drawn, Pop never put pen to paper unless he had to. But a week was given over to preparation, and it consisted of bringing home material for the new shed. All very much secondhand.

He 'obtained' pieces of wood from various friends,. In fact pieces of anything! One day he came staggering home with a friend carrying a large metal advert about four feet by six which said "Camp Coffee is the best". Any spare time was spent hammering bent nails straight; and, he actually bought a few new six inch and four inch nails!

Saturday came, and Pop was up very early, and we awoke to the sound of hammering in the garden. I looked out the window and there was Pop, he had measured out a piece of ground and trampled down the soil to make a floor. He had hammered in six posts on which he was now nailing on odd bits of wood for the walls.

After breakfast I went out eager to help but was told that I should only get in the way, and anyway he wanted no one out in the garden until he was ready to show us the finished shed.

Mid morning tea break was taken by Pop with cold tea as he was too busy to drink it just when it was first handed out from the window. At lunch time he explained to Mum that he would rather have it out side as he had dirty boots, and anyway it was quicker.

Tea time came and the hammering was still going on. Tea was taken at the window with conversation about how hard this had been, and The Blessed thing this and the Blessed thing that! Then back to work. But we could see that 'the shed' had now got a roof on, and he was working on a door for which he was actually screwing in hinges.

The sun was going down in a red ball of flame when Pop came to the door and called "Mum! Come and look at my new shed then, I've finished it."

I moved much faster than Mum and was out into the garden in a flash. Up the path I went, and opened the door. He had even got all the pots of paint on shelves I saw: And In I went.

My first sight was of the bright sunshine making lines of light through the gaps between the bits of wood that made up the wall, and in these lines of red sunshine were floating thousands of bits of dust.

Some of these bits of dust must have got up my nose, for suddenly I let out an enormous sneeze. As I sneezed I must have hit the shelf which was about shoulder height. It came loose somewhere at the far end and tilted downward, the paint pots slid down to hit the wall at the far end like a machine gun, which gave way under the impact so that the end wall went outwards. I turned to make a quick exit, aware as I did so that the wall also was moving outwards and the roof was coming down.

I rushed out on to the path and straight into the arms of Mum and Dad. The sounds of the collapsing roof were still going on, and I was aware that Dad looked extremely cross.

I considered that apologies were due so I came out with the expression that was to be quoted as a family joke for years to come. "I'm sorry Pop, but I only sneezed!"

Mum put her arm round Dad. "Darling, you must admit it's very funny" her words were lost in her laughter. "But my shed" said Dad, but anger was fast disappearing. He went to examine the two sides that had moved outward and the roof which was only now held by one corner. He came back smiling "I suppose I can easily fix it, it just wants a couple of nails on that bit"

After Pop had done his fixing and he had washed and changed he came into the room with a smile. "Was a bit funny, wasn't it!" "Your face was a picture" laughed Mum, "and poor old Gerald.. Sorry Pop, but I only sneezed!"

Chapter 6.

Some people have a very strange and false idea about church. Many think of the church as a building, which of course it is not, the church is people. This idea of a building came about because there have always been so many people coming together to worship God that it would be impossible for them to meet in a house, and as they meet so often they build their own 'tailor made' buildings to suit their needs. People have referred to the church as the place where you will find the people who are the church, meeting together.

To many, 'the church' is a kind of secret society, a people who are some how different from anyone else, they are 'religious', as if there is something abnormal about the spiritual side of man. To yet others church is a kind of organization with faceless people at the top, a kind of 'them and us'; and some parts of the church do look that way, and are supported because some folk like their faith organized that way.

The church that Jesus Christ founded is people, groups of those committed to Him, living for Him and walking with Him. They are, or should be, people who have discovered for themselves that The Creator is a Person who loves and cares, and can be known personally.

I have always felt that the church's biggest problem is it's past. Human beings always hate change, and therefore people will cling to what they have inherited. When you think of it, something that has been going from the dawn of history, like The Christian Faith with it's Old and New Testament background, must be reinterpreted to each new generation, or people will either not understand it, or think that it is irrelevant for their day and age.

God remains the same, and what we know about Him remains the same, but how people accept such truth depends upon how they can sincerely understand it, and make it relevant, for the day in which they live.

There are still groups of Christians (churches) to be found, who talk to God in First Elizabethan English language; goodness knows why! There are still some who try to read The Scriptures in the King James version, where the English words and meanings fail to help any but those schooled in it from childhood.

Also there is the current problem of what to do with large archaic church buildings left by our forefathers, which are totally unsuited to modern man's worship needs: They are a great expense to maintain and heat, Many were built so well that now a preservation order has been placed upon them, which means that they are supposed to be maintained exactly as they are, and which drains the resources of the people that they are supposed to serve. If they are able to be pulled down and rebuilt the cost is almost impossible to find, and questionable as to whether it is right to spend money on this, when there are more worthy causes. Either way, the smaller congregations who use them have an appalling financial burden, at a time of rising inflation.

This creates an outward appearance of the church as an old fashioned, pathetic relic of the past clinging on to something that no one now wants. The truth is that God is knowable, lovable, and wonderful to all who take the trouble to seek Him, this is the real message of the church.

At this time, it seemed I had discovered that there were ways of approaching and worshipping God, other than those of the way in which I had been nurtured, I found delight in a new kind of church and it's fellowship. The old set ways and ideas of my past went! Now I saw that Christianity was a 'Him and me' relationship which was not only exciting and helpful for me but was working out with other people who were also seeking the same thing.

Any coming together of people for a common purpose has to be organized. My teenage revolt was not against God or His people, the Church. It was that it used ideas developed in the days when most people were illiterate. It said in effect "This is the way we have always worshipped, so stand up here, sit down there, say this, do that and you are worshipping God" It did not help me to know God Himself, nor help my weak understanding of Him to grow.

I now see that when I had attended at least two services a Sunday for eight years using the same words, prayers, and forms, it became natural to go through it in parrot fashion, and this to me was insincere. Especially was this so when words and expressions used were misunderstood or of a past generation.

I think that some people love to worship God in this way but it was not for me. My newfound church became like a cold drink of water to a thirsty man. A bit of a shock, but delicious and much needed. Of course every hobby, sport, organization or science has it's jargon words, but here those jargon words I had heard and spoken so ignorantly were explained. I had a new understanding.

I discovered for the first time in my life that God was a person who loved me and cared for me in deeper ways than I could ever plumb. I also found that I could express my feelings to Him in deep commitment, which was rather like a marriage that I knew would last for eternity. I knew what it was to be born all over again, this time as a child of a heavenly Father. I felt like a child who had lived always in poverty on the streets, discovering that I was really the heir of the Lord of The Manor and fabulously rich.

I see now that this new way was the start of something that would give me a new insight into who God was, and understanding of my relationship with Him so that I could start building a new spiritual life.

I was attending this Baptist Church and they had a new Minister, I went to see him with a view to becoming a member of the church. To be part of God's family is vital.

They had no difficulty in recognising me as one committed to Jesus Christ, but they did question whether I was right to join a Baptist Church. I was warmly loved, but sent away to study certain books on Baptist principles and search the scriptures. I returned to the Minister convinced that the Bible did indeed back up what they believed, and I applied not only for membership but also for public Baptism by immersion.

To be baptised and be welcomed as a member of the church was to take longer than usual; there was a war on! All life was difficult. And I did not know that my baptism would never take place in that building, it would be bombed.

The war changed every part of life. In the early days Dad's garden was lost when a gang of workmen came and dug a large whole, followed by others erecting an Anderson Air Raid Shelter, Earth was piled on top, and we built a blast wall in front of it, and made a door to fit the entrance hole.

I well remember the first time we went into it for an air raid, we took down kitchen chairs and sat there. Suddenly Mum said, " I never knew this chair was so low". "Mine is too" I said. We got up to investigate and discovered that our weight had caused the chairs to sink into the earth floor and eight inches of the legs were buried in the soil. Others must have experienced this as well, for soon all shelters were cemented, and later they were reinforced with concrete, floors and sides.

Every night was spent in the air raid shelter in our garden, Being on the direct route for bombers to London we were not to sleep in a bed for the rest of the long war. Each night Mum, Dad, and I would go down into the shelter just before dark where in candle light we would try to read, play games, and eat our meals; while over head the anti-aircraft guns would blaze away and the bombers would drone.

Some times we would sleep through the noises of the night, most of the time we would doze and wake between the German bombing runs. Many times we lay there hearing the bombs whistling down, followed by an ear-splitting explosion and feel the whole shelter rock, and occasionally be thrown from our bunks.

In the early light of dawn we would unbolt the shelter door and creep out all doubled up and stiff one behind the other, looking like some six legge'd monster. Often the sky was red with the glow of many fires. If we thought one of the bombs had been very near we would walk around our local streets to find out where the bomb had dropped. The shock of seeing a friends house nothing more than a pile of rubble never lost it's pain and heart ache no matter how often it happened. I recall the friendly man who called weekly with a supply of paraffin oil from the local ironmongers shop. A land mine had dropped next door to his shop. There was nothing left of the corner pub and five or six shops, but smoking rubble. We would never see his friendly face at our door again or be served in the shop by his wife when we went for the innumerable things that they once sold. From now on we would have to queue up at a shop some way away and carry home our paraffin oil.

So many people that we had known all our lives were suddenly gone. But each bomb that dropped not only killed, it also made many more homeless. The people near the bomb lost everything they had and were lucky to be dug out of the debris alive. For them one had to try to give such little things that one could afford to give them, to help start up a new home; that is if they could get somewhere to live. Many had to move away to live with relations.

Those further from the blast could rescue some of their furniture and personal belongings but had nowhere to put them.

We opened our house to store people's possessions, until they might find somewhere. There at least such things could dry out, being indoors.

People yet further from an incident needed help to board up windows, put doors back on their hinges, and of course the endless sweeping up of glass, and rubble. Falling ceilings make such a mess! The Baptist Minister and I would go round to such needy people and clear the fallen rubble from the damaged furniture and floors. And comfort those suffering from shock.

For some we just had to take over for a while. Find some way to boil some water and make hot sweet tea. Wash the dust and dirt out of their hair. Light a fire in the grate to keep them warm. Talk to them, help them to cry or talk their way through to normality. Some people who had been bombed out several times found it hard to keep a stiff upper lip. They would suddenly and without warning break down into uncontrollable sobbing or hysterical tears as their mind suddenly brought back to reality what they had lived through.

There was one occasion when, walking past a heap of rubble where a bomb had dropped a few days previously, a friend and I thought he heard a noise. We moved about the bombsite listening and then felt sure that we could hear a whimpering noise. The Air-raid Wardens were alerted and the site was opened up again, even though everyone had been accounted for. The result of their digging again into the rubble was the rescue of a medium sized dog.

What to do with him? That was the question, no one claimed him. Mother and I took him in, washed him carefully and dealt with his cuts. We placed him on a blanket and he just lay there and shivered no matter how warm we tried to make him.

I made some enquiries, which eventually led to my visiting an old man in hospital. He was too ill and shocked over the loss of his wife and home to say much but he was pleased to hear that his dog was alive. "Will you have him?" he pleaded "I've nothing left, and can't care for him any more" I asked him what the dog's name was. "We call him 'Crackers', you see he goes crackers every time the air raid warning goes. This will be the fourth time he's been bombed out. I've nothing left in the world now, and no one."

The old man was too low to care about anything, and just too broken. I assured him that we would give his dog a good home and that he could come and see him or have him back at anytime. From what I heard later through he died soon after. Crackers recovered and became our dog.

We had to let the dog out in the garden each night and one night Mother went out to call him in.. "Crackers, Crackers" she called. A policeman walking the road just the other side of our hedge looked over and said "Are you alright madam? I hope you are not referring to me!" She explained that Crackers was the dogs name. He suggested "I should change it's name if I were you".

We thought that this was a good idea so we started to call the dog Bobby. A few nights later when Mother was call-ing the dog in again "Bobby! Bobby!" the same policeman looked over the hedge "You want me, madam?" She once again explained it was the dog's name, and a very confusing conversation took place "I thought it was Crackers" "You said change it, so it's Bobby...." It all ended in laughter as she realised her leg was being pulled.

Bobby/Crackers did go mad and race about terrified when-ever the siren sounded, and there was nothing we could do but cuddle him up. When we were all sleeping down in the shelter, more than once when the noise of battle and bombs were at their height, I have seen him go to each bunk, and with his teeth pull the blanket more fully over each of us, before trembling and shaking he would pull his own blanket over himself and lay quietly whimpering.

I was only fifteen when war started so I was too young for military call up. Later when I was called I was found to be grade four on my medical, largely due to the excessive bleeding complaint I suppose. Anyway, they would not take me.

My brother in the R.A.F. was shipped to Singapore, and when the Japanese took it we were worried for his safety for weeks and weeks. He later told us that three last ships sailed from there. The first was blown out of the water with all on board. The one behind him was bombed and sank. He managed finally to get via various other places to India.

Oh! what a day it was when we heard that he was safe. It was such a relief.

From the earliest days of war I wanted to do something to help in the war effort. I was too young and unfit to join any of the auxiliary services, and my father put his foot down and forbade me to help or do anything to help during air raids.

I wanted to join the A.R.P. (Air Raid Precautions) as a warden, but no matter how I argued he said "no". I know now that he was right, for wherever there was bomb damage there was broken glass and a hundred other things on which I could cut myself, I would probably have been more trouble that I was worth. But I could not see it the then. However, I was determined to do my bit, and as soon as a raid was over

I was off on my bicycle to do what ever I could. Whenever I was out in daylight raids I usually stayed to be as helpful as I could. I volunteered to become dressed up as a casualty for training exercises, and on one occasion I was a casualty on the top floor of a real bombed building. Mock blood and a label telling those who found me what was supposed to be wrong. I was lowered, bound hand and foot to a stretcher from a sixth floor window to the street below. On such occasions prayer comes in very handy indeed I found!

The local ARP Wardens were very sympathetic, and accepted all the help I could give them. During work on an actual bomb incident I was mostly used to run messages and fetch and carry, to stand guard over the dead until the van came to collect them, and sometimes organize mugs of tea to lay the dust.

I sometimes felt that just talking to people or letting them talk was a helpful task alone.

One morning just before dawn I set out on my bike to the wail of the 'All Clear' and headed for the Dartmouth Road, Forest Hill, where the main shops were; I was soon walking over the rubble, passing emergency vehicles, and mixing with the men working on bomb damage and rescue. Then I saw one building, which no one was bothered about standing high above the road. It was 'my Baptist Church'.

I made my way up the rubble-strewn steps and past the doors, now blown off and at crazy angles in the entranceway. It was just getting light, and as I entered the church I looked up to see a star where once the roof had been. The pews were covered with ceiling plaster and bits of timber.

The nearest window had a large piece of the glass hanging dangerously suspended by a single piece of lead and gently swinging in the dawn breeze. I could see that this could easily fall on someone, so I decided to get up and remove it.

Pushing plaster and rubble from the pew I clambered on to the pew seat and broke the leaded section away with a twist and eased the chunk of window to the floor. As I put my hand onto the windowsill to steady myself for the decent, a jagged sliver of glass fell from somewhere above and imbedded itself into my right hand pointer finger knuckle. I still bear the scar today to remind my how I bled like a pig for hours that morning.

I cycled to the Church Secretary's home and broke the news to Frank that our beloved church building was badly damaged. It could not be used during the rest of the war, so the church moved into the church hall at the back. That hall was to be the centre of my life, the place of social events and parties, church meetings and Sunday worship.

Now, with only a hall, it became a rule of the church that Saturday events like parties had to stop before midnight, and it seemed strange to me how we could be having a wonderful time dancing or playing games on a Saturday night, perhaps shouting and dancing the 'Okey-Cokey', and then suddenly it would come to an end, an army of people would be sweeping up, chairs put in rows, Communion Table, a Pulpit and flowers would appear, and in next to no time it would be our church, and all ready for Sunday worship.

Somehow it brought sacred and secular together in a unique way that seemed so right in one way, but wrong in another. I had been brought up to think of 'God's House' as sacred. You didn't run there, or talk above whispers; now I felt bewildered, could I still worship with the same feelings?

I found that I could. The atmosphere of church worship filled that little hall on Sundays, We still worshipped God, He still spoke to us and helped us.

In talking to people within the church I discovered that there were not only the different denominations I had already discovered, but different ways of thinking within the denominations. In the Church of England I had seen what was known as 'High' and 'Low' churches. Anglo-Catholics worshipping with incense and candles like Roman Catholics. in contrast to those whose churches were plain and the worship more simple.

Now I discovered that there were Modernists and Evangelicals. People in the church had strong feelings about this. As I did not like 'old fashioned' things I decided I would be a Modernist, and when one visiting Minister was called a Modernist I looked for what would make him so.

I decided that it was his modern hair style with very liberal use of hair cream, and his many illustrations in the sermon.

How wrong and ignorant can one be?

I did discover something during those days of worship in the church hall which few Christians ever discover. That Buildings are not important to faith. Whatever affection you might have for your church building, even if your parents and grand-parents were married there, or it has very happy memories. It makes no difference to your relationship with God. If it is pulled down, or you move to another area, God is always the same, and one can always make new friends. In these days when so many church buildings are closing and so many new ones being built it is good to know that it will make no difference to the real situation between a person and their God.

Out of all this change I also learned, to my surprise, the Great Secret that the church is commissioned to tell everyone, and which it sometimes seems to be ashamed to talk about is that That God's way to save people is so easy and simple, and is available to everyone who will have it. It is a free gift from God.

If you have ignored someone or had no relationship with them you have to do something about it. With God you tell Him how sorry you really are about the past and that you want to start now being close friends. You ask Him to take over your life and run it for you because you make too many mistakes and He does everything perfectly. If you've asked Him to forgive your past, He has done it! So say "Thank you", and accept His forgiveness as a fact. If you have asked Him to take over your life, He has done so, say "Thank you" and co-operate with Him from now on. Talk to Him all the time in your mind, He hears you. Listen to thoughts that he will put in your mind, He will talk to you. Practice this day by day until it becomes the natural thing to do all the time.

Start reading the Bible. One of the Gospels first perhaps, then the New Testament, before the Old Testament. Link up with others who are also following Him so that you can learn together and have support. Really church-going has nothing to do with being good or doing your duty. It is joining with others who are also following Him so that you can express better your praise and thanksgiving, learn from Him, and band together to practise loving Him and other people.

For me, there was no hope now of my being baptised in my own bomb-damaged church building, but the Minister was finally able to arrange it at a church some miles away, in Brownhill Road Baptist Church, Catford.

The Minister there was a saintly white haired man named Rev: A.H.Hawkins. He had several people from his own church who were going to be baptised that night, and I arrived with many friends on Sunday 21st September 1947. The church was vast, and packed from floor to gallery.

Before the service we candidates for baptism were told that if we wished to speak to the congregation before going down into the water we should feel free to do so, but to keep it brief and speak out loud so that all could hear.

The service was an impressive one, the sermon heart warming, and singing loud and enthusiastic. The time for baptism came and three others before me walked to the baptistery, down the steps chest high in water and were immersed following the pronouncement "I Baptise you in the name of the Father, and of Jesus The Son, and of The Holy Spirit". They were then guided to the exit steps and received by helpers with towels and taken to dry off and don dry clothing. I walked to the side of the pool and spoke in a loud clear voice. I told the crowded church that I had accepted Christ as my Saviour when a boy, and that He had not ceased to guide me all the way to this point where I was now publicly professing my faith. I went on to say words that just seemed to come into my mouth. I was called of God to serve Him all my days, and that my Lord had a work for me to do of which I knew nothing at that moment. My life was not going to be easy, but it would be satisfying in His service, and one day I would see Him face to face and enjoy Him forever.

I went down into the water with a strange mixture of fear and joy. Fear because I had never been under water before, joy from a sense of spiritual uplift.

I stood in the water, hands clasped and body straight, as instructed. I heard the words of baptism, a hand on my chest pushed me backwards, an arm supported my back, I watched the water close over me, the lights of the church dancing above me, then I was coming up again... coughing and spluttering in a most impious way. I tried to stop the noise I was making but all to no avail. I was helped out, warm towels mopping my face. On such a sacred moment why did I have to spoil it by coughing and spluttering in that most undignified way? The service was soon over and I have memories of dozens of friends and unknown people warmly shaking my hand and blessing me. Later the Minister appeared with the same warm greeting, then he added, I hoped that you would not talk too long, what you did not know was that I had a hole in my waders and the water was slowly creeping coldly up my legs.

There was a great shortage of preachers during the war days. Some Ministers had joined the forces as chaplains, most of the men were away fighting, and there were very few women who preached. I had been a lay preacher since I was about fifteen, and now felt that I should continue to take services and preach So I had accepted what training my Minister could give me as to how to lead in worship and preach The Gospel, and well remember my first preaching engagement to conduct the evening service at Cottage Green Baptist Church Camberwell. London.

It was a cold night and the rain was driving down. As always I arrived at the church nearly half an hour too early with family and a couple of friends.

When finally the church was opened I was ushered into the Minister's Vestry where I was able to stand in front of a roaring coal fire. I entered the pulpit and began the service, but I could not stop shaking with nerves and the cold. There was a small electric bowl fire at my feet and steam rose from my soaking trousers. However, as the worship proceeded I began to feel the warmth moving up my body. By the time I got to the sermon I had lost my shakes and announced my text. Revelation 3v20. "Behold I stand at the door and knock".

Later on in life when I saw those sermon notes again I marvelled that I could ever say such things, and winced at this early effort; but it was a first effort, without proper training, and it did have the ring of sincerity. At least I had started, and everyone gave me warm encouragement.

So I then began to preach in churches in and around London, and my own church at Sydenham did not see me attending every Sunday, although I did preach there from time to time.

Whenever someone gets close to God or starts to serve Him it always seems to annoy Satan and make him try to pull that person down, and his ways are so subtle. His attack on me now was to build up so slowly and look so innocent that I neither saw it coming or dreamed that I was in any danger.

One day when calling in at the church I met a lady who was at that time acting as caretaker, and I was introduced to her daughter Jane, who had come along with her. "I found her very attractive," something clicked between us from that very first meeting and my life was to take on a new exciting phase.

I had learned ballroom dancing at the Forsyd Youth Club and greatly enjoyed both the dancing and the dance music. Having learned from the famous Frank and Peggy Spencer I enjoyed doing fancy steps, but sadly there was no one that I knew that was a really good dancer. Now Jane asked me if I were going to the dance on Saturday and the outcome was that I took her as my partner.

The dance was a huge success. She was a better dancer than I was, and we had great fun together teaching each other different steps. She was such good fun to be with, and life became a happy round of laughter and we both enjoyed going out and about, and to dance after dance.

Strangely, it never occurred to me that I was falling for her in a big way. She was so friendly by nature that it seemed natural to go about arm in arm, and kiss 'goodnight', and all this was a new and great experience for me. For I had never really had a girl friend before. I think that we both thought of our relationship as a wonderful friendship, and we felt free to talk about anything without reserve, and did most of the time!

She wanted to know about my Christian Faith, confessing that she was a Communist. I at once saw it as my mission to bring her to know my Lord. She said that she did not know all the answers that her Communist Party would have against my faith, and finally it was agreed that I should attend her Communist Party Meeting as Guest Speaker to give my views and experience of the Christian faith, and that they would have the opportunity of questioning me after.

I jumped at what I saw as the chance to convert the Communist Party and the date was arranged.

How naive I was. They gave me a good hearing, and I explained how I had found God to be a real and wonderful friend who had the desire and power to care for His people. Afterward their questions and comments were about 'The Church', it's money and property, its failings, and old fashioned mumbo jumbo. They were polite, but both sides left each convinced that right was on our own side.

Jane seemed to be moving closer to my beliefs and I saw as much of her as I could. We went everywhere together, sometimes like bosom pals, sometimes like a romantic couple. The day came when I suddenly faced the fact that Jane meant more to me than anyone else I had met, that she was my girlfriend, and I might one day even marry her. I was about to have the biggest shock of my young life.

It was Saturday and we were as usual at a dance. There was always a number of men in uniform at the dances and this night was no exception. As we finished a dance and returned to our seat Jane said "Seeing all these soldiers makes me wonder about my husband, I haven't heard from him for three weeks".

At first I though she was joking, then there was a look between us and she became as shocked as I. "You knew I was married, didn't you?" I was trembling as I said "No!". She looked concerned "Frank is in the army, I thought you knew".

We left the dance although it was early, I took her home, but would not hold her arm, she belonged to someone else, she was married. Jane was baffled, "I've written and told Frank all about you and the fun we have together". she sounded upset

"I told him you are the best friend I ever had... he's looking forward to meeting you when he comes home on leave".

We walked to her Mum's house where she lived. She refused to let me go until we had sorted out our relationship. She explained that we were close friends, she enjoyed my friendship and could see nothing wrong or wicked in walking arm in arm with me, or kissing me. She loved me very much as a friend and someone she could trust while her husband was away. She was young and wanted to go out with someone who was upright and trustworthy, she did not want to lock herself up in one room and never go out, and she had come to even thank God for my friendship and the fun we enjoyed.

She was a great talker in her quiet way. She put forward the thought that may be it was part of God's will for both of us, God forbid that Frank should be killed in action, but if that were to be she would need a good friend like me at such a time, for she had no one else. Who knows what the future might hold for both of us she argued.

I was only too willing to see her reasoning, and we parted on the firm understanding that we should continue our friendship as if nothing had happened. She was loyal to Frank, and when we kissed it would be enjoyable to both of us but it was as very wonderful friends. In the coming days my mind had many battles. I would shock myself by telling myself that I was going out with a married woman. Then I would think what a great friendship we had and how we would share it with her husband. I was also hoping and praying that she would become a Christian, there were times when she seemed so near it!. Then Frank came home on leave, they went everywhere together, and I spent one evening with them both. Frank and I were poles apart, he actually called me 'Sir' on one occasion. He accepted that we were very good friends and that there was nothing between us. I suspected that he wished that I wasn't going to be around his wife, friend or no friend. For my part I wondered why she had married him and suspected that she had more fun with me than with him. Which was sheer conceit of my part.

It seemed that he had no objection to my helping his wife to enjoy life. He took her view that she was young and needed to go out, he said he would rather her go out with me than go by herself, or with someone she did not know. It seemed that we would continue in our friendship.

Chapter 7.

Privately my thoughts were turning more and more to what God would have me do in life. I still wandered from job to job hoping to find what I was supposed to do with life, and I still found nothing suitable.

I turned my attention to charitable work and I applied to the famous Dr Barnardo's Homes who were looking for a House Master. I had an interview at their head quarters in Stepney, and I was offered a place in a children's evacuation home in Norfolk. After much prayer and soul searching I accepted it for two reasons. One was that it just MIGHT be what God wanted me to do with my life, and Secondly that I wanted to get away from Jane who was allowing me and even encouraging me to kiss and hold her too often, and I wasn't sure it was right. I caught the train to Norfolk and settled in as House Master at their temporary Home in the village of Marham.

The boys were a happy lot in spite of the regimentation of a 'home' life.

I woke them in the morning, supervised their dressing, and breakfast, marched them to the little village school, and collected them after, helping them with their spare-time activities. They were all different, and responded in various ways, and I soon got the hang of being a House Master.

There were times when I reasoned that I was only very ordinary, in fact rather poorly educated with no degrees or examination results: To give my life to poor children would be a life's work well suited to someone like me. Perhaps this was what God was calling me to be. Then I would feel completely convinced that there was something else that The Lord was wanting me to do and that I was in the wrong job ,I was no good at sport and rush-about games with the children, and not much help to them with their home work from school. I should go back to London.

Meanwhile, life with the boys continued day by day. One of the threats I heard the other 'Masters' use on the boys, made me curious. They often laughingly said "If you don't behave, Sister Barbara will get you".

"What's this Sister Barbara stuff" I asked. "Oh I suppose you don't know" came the answer. "This old house and grounds was once a Convent, and the locals say that one of the Nuns, Sister Barbara, committed suicide here. They say that it was so against her beliefs and vows that she cannot rest, and that from time to time she is seen usually in the house but sometimes in the grounds; a walking ghost". When I tell you of my experience of Sister Barbara I think you will be amused, but it was not funny to me as a young lad all alone in the 'haunted house!'

The Americans had an Air Base just up the road from the Home and when some of the service men there discovered that there was an orphanage near by they became quite generous in little gifts of food stuffs for the boys. They came with 'candy' and a few toys, and some of the food that we just couldn't get in war time. None of the staff ever had any benefit from such generosity, but there was one thing in which we did share the enjoyment. Our boys were given the offer to attend their weekly film show, and every Thursday night the staff walked the boys to the Air Base for a free picture show.

However, rules of the Home made it essential that one of the staff stay in the house while the rest went, so we Housemasters all took it in turns to be caretaker for the Thursday evening shows. My turn came, and I might have forgotten about ghosts if one of the boys had not called out as they left "Goodbye, we shan't see you again, Sister Barbara 'll get you".

I settled down in the lounge, with a roaring coal fire, a good book, and a "ghosts? bah! humbug!" attitude. It was a draughty old house and the door was just behind my armchair, so I pulled a large old screen around the chair and settled down. The wind was getting up and began to howl round the house, but I was well into my book and hardly noticed it.

Suddenly there was a crash from upstairs. I looked at the time, it was far too early for them to return and I wondered whether someone had come back not feeling well..

I ascended the big staircase and searched for the cause of the crash. The boys had not left the rooms very tidy in their excitement to dress for the film show so it could have been any thing on the floor. At that moment I heard a noise downstairs and hastened to the top of the stairs. I was just in time to see something white disappear through the doorway.

I went cold! Sister Barbara! I thought. I paused to think, then ran down the stairs with as much noise as I could. As I reached the doorway the white appeared again, and I saw that it was the inner lining of the curtain, and the window was partly open. I shut it firmly.

The house now seemed to be filled with creaks and noises, and I made a detailed inspection of every room in the house. Looking from one upstairs window I saw Sister Barbara gliding across the lawn, on closer inspection it turned out to be a white paper bag in the wind. I returned to my armchair and noticed that my heart was hammering away so much that I could only read my book with difficulty. Every noise was noted, every gust of wind was heard and twice I left my room convinced that I heard someone on the stairs outside.

I checked the time, it would be at least twenty minutes before the house again resounded to chatting House Masters and little boys, I resolved to ignore all sounds and read my book. For a good five minutes I read, conscious of the wind rattling the door and howling around. Then it happened! There was a loud moan of high wind, the door flew open, and the screen collapsed on top of me striking me smartly on the head. I let out a yell, got out of the screen draped chair in panic and rushed through the open door scared out of my wits! I went to the front door and opened it, hoping to see the returning party, it was too early. It took me five minutes to gather enough courage to go back inside, to right the screen and restore my jaded nerves. I had worked myself into a state of mind where I was scared and I felt a real fool. I was so glad to have them all return, though I would not have told them so.

I learned much from my time in the Home. These children had all that any child could have, toys, companions, good food, and every comfort. But they lacked the one thing that every one of them would have given everything to have – Love! Nearly all of them were there because their parents were divorced, or could not, or would not have them. We gave them what love we could, but it was not the love they wanted.

I think that the American servicemen came nearest to giving them some love. They came as visitors because they wanted to come. They hugged them and played with them, and gave little gifts.

Several of the children had a fantasy that they shared with you in great secrecy. Next week a Mum, or Uncle, or someone, was coming to take them home. They never came of course, but the hope was always there. Some had special private possessions which they only rarely showed a trusted friend such as their house master. One boy had a tobacco tin and his greatest possession in it was a stone. I asked him why the stone was of importance to him. He paused, then said in a low awed voice " I saw my dad tread on this stone when he left me last time". That would have been two years before. The father would never come and see him again but that boy worshipped him just the same. There was the boy who was playing 'house' as he called it. He was far from the others behind some bushes on the other side of the grounds. He was Father, and there was an imaginary Mother who he was rowing with and calling all the names he could think of. He was acting out what he could remember of his early home life. In talking it out with the Head it was discovered that he thought that all home life was father and mother fighting and name calling. It was all he could remember of it. He knew no better.

Jane often telephoned me at the home. She must have spent quite a lot on those long phone calls. She gave me the news that when Frank had been on leave they had visited the housing department and she had been fortunate enough to have a small two room flat allocated to her. She had moved from her mother's home, and now she wanted me to come and see it. She seemed to have an answer and way around all my excuses in those conversations. "You ought to visit your Mother anyway, come back for a week end".

It is emotionally stunning for a young man who thinks he's in love, to hear the girl say "Of course I can't hide the fact that I'm in love with you as much as you know you are in love with me" But this is what she would tell me. "I can't help my feelings for you, come back home, we can see each other again...I want you". It was all very tempting but I remained firm. She was married and that was that! Another phone call told me that Frank was on his way overseas, how nice it would be if I, her only real friend, came and comforted her.

Meanwhile, life at the Home was not so good. I scalded my hand early one morning while making the early morning tea. No one was around to help me and I was in great pain having poured the kettle of boiling water on my hand instead of in the pot which I had been holding. I prayed for help, and even as I prayed I wondered if this might be God saying either, keep away from Jane, or more likely leave here this is not where I want you.

Of course these ideas were all rubbish, God does not do things like that. To my further prayer I was surprised to have the pain go within half an hour, and the scald marks disappear within the morning. An interview with the Head of the Home, planned from the beginning of my work with Barnardo's took place during that same period; his searching questions left me in no doubt that I was not going to stay in

Long Road To The Manse

this kind of work. I said I would think and pray the matter over, but in my heart I knew then that I must leave soon.

My Mother phoned and I shared my thoughts with her and she too counselled me to come home.

Then Jane phoned "I'm not just saying this to get you back to me" she said "I really do have something very important and urgent I want to share with you, can you possibly come?". I told her 'yes', packed my bags and said my goodbyes. All the way home on that long train journey I was wondering what Jane had to tell me that was so urgent and important. The only thing I feared was that she had received bad news about her husband. This kind of news was so common at that time, it seemed the only answer. I would visit her and see her new flat and find out what the trouble was as soon as I could; After all that was what friendship was all about.

Looking back I can now see how innocent and naive I was. I had been praying that she would accept Christ as Lord and Saviour and thought that my visit, whatever her news, would be a perfect opportunity to talk to her about it. If I had affection for her it would be always as a friend and I was not going back to taking her out and treating her like a girl friend. As I made my way to her new flat, these thoughts filled my mind.

She opened the door and with a gushing smile brought me in. As soon as the door was shut she threw herself into my arms, pressing her body to mine. I held her tightly thinking that she needed some comfort, perhaps she had received the fateful telegram. She said nothing for some time but pressed her kisses upon my cheek and made my face wet with her tears. Then through her gasps and little noises she started to say things.

"You know I love you" "I am yours completely" "I've wanted you to have me for so long and now at last it's going to happen" I relaxed my hold as I tried to decipher what she was saying. She misunderstood my relaxing grip and stood back a little saying "The settee is very comfortable." then." No, Darling, you haven't seen my lovely little bedroom, have you."

I grabbed her hand and stopped her, I stood for a moment looking at her. The look on her face told me that I had not misunderstood her. The top buttons of her dress were undone, she looked more desirable than I had ever seen any girl look before. I had never seen an unclothed woman, and I shamelessly looked at her figure, wanting to see her like that now. I had never made love in that way ever before, and now I wanted to with every fibre of my being. No girl had ever offered herself like this before. I experienced an urge to take her in my arms again with passion rather than sympathy. I could feel my resistance going, and I liked the feeling. A little thought whispered 'It's really going to happen.' My cheeks went hot and my whole body tingled.

"NO" I thought "it is wrong" "Sex outside marriage is wrong for me, and adultery is wrong for her. 'O God,' in my mind I prayed 'please, NO!' "Stop me!". It was as if I was held in a kind of limbo for a moment and then another thought came unbidden into my mind. "What ever would your Mother say if you did this?".

That was enough! I loved my Mother too much to hurt her, and it would break her heart. I loved God too much to hurt Him, and He had plainly said 'no' to this.

"Jane," I mumbled, pulling her back toward the settee. "We can't do this it's wrong". Her whole attitude changed in an instance. "Don't be silly darling" she scolded "Come and sit here, I told you I've got something important to tell you".

We sat on the settee. She was finding it difficult "I don't want you to look at me while I tell you... Put your arm around me... and your head on my shoulder". She paused, and I waited "You know when Frank was on embarkation leave?" she paused, again searching for words, "It must have happened then.. I'm going to have a baby." My mind reeled and then went blank, I did not know what to say. She turned toward me, slowly kissing my cheek. "So you see darling," she was coaxing with her voice, "it's all right, you can make love to me, we can enjoy one another, all the way, as we've never done ". "You want to have me, don't you"?

I didn't know anything about women and babies, but I got the last bit of the message. For one moment the thought of us being together here and now brought back all my burning desires. She leant over me and kissed me long and lingering. The desire to put my arms around her was difficult to resist, and then she took my hand and led it toward her undone buttons.

I pulled away roughly. "NO" I said "it's wrong, we both know it". "It's not" she countered almost angrily "We both want to love each other. It can't harm anyone, no one will ever know, and our love can be fulfilled as it should be". "Just Once!" She pleaded, as she looked at me "You do love me... I know you do, Don't you! .." My mind seemed to be tearing down the middle. "Then show me, love me now". I couldn't think straight. I found myself saying in an angry tone "Oh all right then"

Even as I said it I had to follow it with "No, I won't.. maybe .." I struggled for words "I respect and even love you.. too much to do this, but you are Frank's, and I won't commit adultery with you." I got up from the settee "I'm happy for you both about the baby". I didn't know what I was saying now, but I knew I had to run away quick, or I would give in. "If there is anything else I can do.. as a friend.." Her voice came hard "At the moment, JUST GO!". she said. I walked to the door and closed it quickly behind me, never to return.

Human nature took over as I walked home. Any other man would have jumped at the chance I told myself. It could have really happened. She wanted it to happen. The battle raged in my mind. 'I could still go back to her'. 'No it's wrong.' 'Everyone does it'. 'No they don't!' Finally I said out loud under my breath "When God says 'no' that's good enough, He knows best, so that is the end of the matter". I returned home feeling dirty, I recall washing and washing, and feeling extremely tired. When I went to bed early my mother thought that I was unwell and was most concerned. If only I could have told her that she, and thoughts of her had saved me.. but she would never know.

I found that it took a long time to get over that encounter, but I never regretted the stand I had made and was again and again thankful to God who had supplied the thought that stopped me. I now dreaded that I would meet Jane in the street sometime. Twice I saw her in the distance while shopping and deliberately avoided her.

Again and again I wondered whether she would have told me that the baby was her husband's if I had fallen into the temptation of that day, would she have tried to tell me it was mine? Would I have ever known for sure? She might have told me that it was mine, divorced her husband and got me to marry her, and my whole future would have changed forever. That decision could have changed my life's course.

My prayers of thanksgiving were more real and sincere every day. It was not sinful to have been tempted, and I felt so happy that I had been helped to resist and say 'no'. But what a fool I had been to put myself in that position in the first place.

Months later I received a long letter from her with the news that she was in the hospital, and that she and Frank had a daughter. The full details of the birth were all there, the little girl had been born feet first and was therefore bound to be a wonderful dancer like her mother, who with the right partner could be in heaven on the dance floor.

For months I had bottled up the flaming memory of my encounter, with no one I could share it with, nor could I share it until now. This chapter in my life was now closed I told myself firmly, I just hoped I had learned a valuable lesson, and that I could forget the flame that so often burnt in my mind with more lust than love.

Now that I was back home from the Dr. Barnardo's home, I was without a job, and it had been a long time since I had been with my friends. The next day dawned with Sunday worship in the Baptist hall. Every one seemed pleased to see me, and in no time I was back in the old routine and happy to be so.

The Labour Exchange told me that the local Radio and Electrical shop needed a trainee electrician so I had to apply. Having some knowledge of electricity which I had acquired from my brother, I was happy to try the job, was this what God had for my future?. That first Monday morning I was introduced to the 'electrician' who would have charge of me, and he asked if I could repair the domestic appliances that were awaiting repair on the bench. I said I would have a go, so he left me to it.

Being my first day I should have been aware of possible pranks, but I didn't notice the two probes left, one on the bench and one on the nearest domestic iron. My hand must has been resting on the metal part of the bench as I went to pick up the iron.. I never quite knew whether I jumped with surprise or the electric shock threw me, but I went backwards hitting a stack unit of spare parts, nuts, bolts and bits and pieces, it gave way to my onslaught, and the following twenty minutes was spent in sorting out the mess.

I had little trouble in replacing elements in irons and kettles, but when I came to the radio with a note on it "Won't work" I plugged it in and switched it on, with luck it might only be a broken connection in the lead or plug. I waited for the set to warm up, peering into the back to see if the valves were heating up. There was a Flash and Bang, and my face was covered with smuts and dirt. I saw where the smoke was coming from, so I wrote a note "Suggest new transformer". and left it.

They thought that I was rather slow at repairing toasters and irons: And I heard the boss tell the customer in the shop about his radio, "You can't get the staff during wartime".

So I was sent out to work on house wiring, a difficult thing in wartime with shortages of proper cable and equipment. I hated getting up into lofts, walking only on the joists fearing putting my foot through the ceiling: Crawling under floors with a torch or candle was not my idea of a God given calling. I did my best, but it was obvious to me that I was not going to make an electrician and I managed to get my self sacked after a few weeks in order that I could return to the Labour Exchange for another job without being shouted at and earn their displeasure.

I felt some excitement as I waited at the job counter. Would this next job be the work I was destined to do for the rest of my life? Perhaps they had work in some kind of Charity or Christian organization, and I would work up to know the whole business and one day contribute in some special way to the welfare of all mankind. The clerk thumbed through the cards and finally pulled one out. "Longhurst Welders are looking for someone, go along and see them" he said, writing out the green card. So off I went.

Longhurst Welders turned out to be a small factory-like building with much dirt, noise, and smoke. As I entered, men were banging metal, welding, soldering tin boxes, and operating machines. I sat in the office for sometime before being interviewed. They did not seem interested in my character or appearance as other employers had, in fact the whole interview was over in a flash, and I was told to start on Monday. When I asked what I would be doing, I was told "Well, you don't know anything, and have no experience so you'll have to learn and work hard.

I was taught how to file metal, hammer things, and work machines. Clad in a blue bib and brace overall which became filthy in no time, I cut my fingers often, and spent my evenings pulling out splinters of steel from my hands, and treating bruises. The only happy spot in each day was the mid-morning break when I would be sent with another lad to the local baker's shop for Banbury cakes which were warm and fresh from the oven, and more delicious than I had ever tasted before or since.

I had been there for a few weeks when a well dressed man, whom I had taken to be one of the bosses, and who visited the factory for a brief period on most days, came up to me. He had a special job for me grinding down rivets on dozens of boxes. He showed me how to operate the grinding machine and left me to it.

The noise of that job almost deafened me, even after I had obtained some cotton wool from the first aid box to put in my ears. It set my teeth on edge and I hated it. But it seemed to be important to the 'boss' so I went at it with a will, working as quickly as I could possibly go.

After a little time the 'boss' returned and motioned that I should shut off the machine. I removed the cotton wool from my ears, but still found it difficult to hear what he was saying. I said I was sorry that I couldn't hear very well, it was the noise that seemed to deafen me. "Do you like this work?" he asked "No not really" I replied "Why is that?" he retorted "I suppose it's not what I'm used to, I'm only used to office work." "Would you rather do clerical work?" "Yes" I replied. "Come with me" he demanded, and walked out of the little shop in which I had been grinding.

After the man had spoken to the foreman and one of the other bosses he returned to me. "Take your overalls off, pick up you coat and anything else of yours and wait for me outside", he commanded. I did so. Soon he was briskly striding out of the works, ordering me into his car and driving me away. "I'm Mr Tooley, do you know my garage?" "No sir" "I sell and service motorbikes at my garage, do you know anything about motorbikes?" "No sir".

The drive was brief, and we swung into a small yard way with a shop and workshop. Three new motorbikes were on display in the shop window, and a man was sitting on the floor of the workshop repairing a motorbike.

Tooley's Garage sold and serviced Velocette Motorcycles, and I was shown around the workshop, the spares store, and the office. "How would you like to work here?" I was asked "I could use someone to order spares, see to customers and do general jobs here in the office". My hearing was coming back and I heard this offer loud and clear, anything was better than the noisy dirty workshop. "Would the wages be the same?" I asked "I'll pay you what you get now, and we will see how it works out". He looked seriously at me "You may not like this job either".

From that moment onward I worked for Mr Tooley. It took some time to learn the names for various parts of the motorbikes, and their part numbers, to know what to order and the suppliers, also to get to know the customers.

I made some mistakes, like ordering for stock parts that were rarely used, and dropping a drawer full of nuts and bolts which took most of a day to resort and put back into the drawer. I did a stocktaking which turned out disastrously and had to be done all over again, and I left the boss's push bike outside where it was stolen. But other things worked out well and won me some commendations. I found the mechanic a nice enough chap to get on with, he was a real motorbike fanatic and travelled on his own machine through all weathers.

Mr Tooley was a fair man to work for and he raised my pay a few weeks after I started there. I made myself take an interest in the work, but I wondered more and more what the future held if I stayed as office junior in a small motor-bike garage. I felt restless, and experienced an urgent almost panic-like desire to find what I thought of as my real work in life. This was not it and I knew it. I turned to the Local Newspapers jobs column and was intrigued at one advert which read 'Wanted. Young man, polite and of neat appearance seeking life work in the boot and shoe industry. There followed an address and phone number of a shoe shop in near by Lewisham. I made an appointment and went.

The Manager of the shoe shop took me to a cramped office behind the shop and I was aware that he was looking over my appearance. He asked "What made you apply to our advert?" "I suppose it was the 'life-time' bit. In a shoe shop?" I questioned. He gazed at me as he asked "Do you know how often people have to buy new shoes or boots?". I pondered the question "About every two or three years?". "And do you know how many people live in Britain?" was his next question. I had to smile at his seriousness and questions "I've never thought of counting them". I grinned. Without a smile he came back at me "56 million people, and they buy around 30 million pairs of working shoes a year".

I wondered just where this was leading, until his next statement. "30 million pairs of shoes this year, and the same next year, and the next.. for as long as you or I live they will want and need shoes and boots.". He looked down at my feet "You are wearing black Oxfords about size eight, and you will need to replace them within six months, what would you do if there were no shoes to buy... anywhere? " He paused for effect

"Everybody HAS to have footwear. And most people have more than one pair of walking shoes, plus Working Boots, Sunday best, Shoes for dancing, Running and Games; shoes for Riding, Gumboots, Slippers.. the need is far greater than you think. Children grow out of theirs, women have to have them to match outfits and be in fashion."

"The war won't last for ever lad, and then there will be new fashions, colours and styles. Every time the people come for shoes there will be someone helping them, serving them, showing them. It is the greatest service you can give to your fellow human beings, supplying something they urgently need."

I had never seen a shoe shop in this light before, and as I was obviously impressed he spent another twenty minutes or so talking about the design, manufacture, and distribution of boots and shoes. If I joined them it would be because I did not just want a job in shop work but a career in the industry, and I would learn all about it and be properly trained in their company. So I Joined Them! True to the manager's word I was taught about leather, the parts of the shoe, how they were made, and the various styles and fittings. I was trained how to sit at the feet of customers and ensure their satisfaction in footwear; how to affix rubber soles and heels to increase the length of life of the shoe, and how to advise about shoe repairs and send them off with right instructions.

I found great satisfaction in the knowledge I was given and in the way I could talk to customers about their feet and the best footwear for them. I was able to stretch shoes especially for folk with bunions, and felt myself becoming an authority on 'my subject'. Then the old feeling started again, it was a feeling that I was wasting precious time kneeling before people's smelly feet in order to sell them shoes. Whether I was a good shoe salesman or not the industry would continue to prosper and make and sell shoes. There WAS something else I had to do. I felt certain of it.

I would kneel and pray, sit and pray, and lie in bed and pray. I would scan my bible, and sometimes even share my feelings with trusted fellow Christians, but no guidance seemed to come. One friend said that I should push every door in life until one opened. I decided to try that.

There were various Christian Charities and organizations, and I made some appointments to discuss whether my call might lie with them. Each such appointment was proceeded by my prayers for guidance but the only guidance I felt was 'NO' to each one.

On one occasion I had an appointment at an important gentleman's house.

I arrived half an hour early and walked the street waiting for the appointed hour. When at last I rang the door bell a maid ushered me into the hall. She entered the large lounge room to tell the great man I had arrived, and she motioned me in.

The wooden floor was highly polished, I stepped on to a mat just inside the doorway and it slipped from under me sending me crashing to the floor, I ended up at the great man's feet, confused, embarrassed, and hurting like mad.

The great man helped me to my feet, and in my embarrassment I said the first daft thing that came into my head. I said "Enter the fairy tripping lightly". His apologies and enquiry "Did you hurt yourself?" were met with my "No, that's alright". But it was only with great self-control that I could prevent myself from rubbing the painful parts all through the interview, and I was thinking so much about my entrance that I could not concentrate on the matter I had waited so urgently to discuss.

One promising contact brought me to explore the work of the British Sailors Society. They had places in every port in the world so that sailors had a place to 'hang their hat' where ever they were. They provided port missioners to help sailors and also stocked the ship libraries. There is no doubt that they do a wonderful work among both sailors and their dependants in so many ways.

Not only did I spend time in their hostel in the Commercial Road, but on one memorable day I went aboard a ship in the docks with a Missionary to take a service and communion. The large cabin set aside for us was filled with merchant sailors both white and coloured. I went round with hymn books, and as soon as the service started I noticed that others were crowding the steps that led on deck. I went up these steps giving out hymns books, and as I got to the top I paused and found that two other ships moored across the harbour had sailors also joining in the singing. The strange sound of that hymn from men across the water and near at hand has come back to me often when I have sung it in various churches since. Under many a rough exterior there is a sensitive spirit.

From the British Sailors Society I learned to play games, watch films and talk with these tough men of the sea. Underneath there was a warm hearted person who from time to time would open up to reveal love and tragedy. But I seemed to feel so helpless in the face of their needs. Maybe it was all experience for some future calling but I knew this too was not the way for me.

Perhaps I ought to look to myself and what I would like to do. I sat down to think it through and came up with the answer that I liked cars, and had a driving licence which did not get very much use, so I decided to try my hand at being a motor mechanic.

I applied to a big Ford dealer garage in Lewisham and was engaged as a trainee mechanic. I arrived on a cold Monday morning and stood around the big pot-bellied stove and watched the others warming their overalls and putting them on. I was then supplied with overalls with leg length far too long, and allocated to a mechanic who every one call Revvie.

"Come on kid" he suddenly said and I followed him to the breakdown truck. I climbed into the passenger seat with great difficulty, being so short, and we drove down the main streets of Lewisham and Lee as if we were a fire engine. We finally turned off into a very small alley between a row of shops, descended a sharp lane and came out into a yard with various vehicles dotted about. I read the advert on the side of the lorries 'Rely on Lion Cartage'. Revvie left the truck and spoke to a foreman, returning with the command "Out you get kid". He led me to a long eight wheeled vehicle which had a bonnet and cab but no body, only a very long chassis. It was to be towed to the garage to have a body built on it and an engine put in.

"Ever done a tow before?" he asked "No". "Well get in the cab". I climbed up with difficulty and seated myself in the driver's seat. I was sitting behind the biggest steering wheel I had ever seen, and I could only see out of the windscreen only through the spokes of the steering wheel, or by standing up.

Revvie turned and backed the tow truck in front of my cab. Fixing the old bit of rope between to two vehicles, he came and looked in the cab doorway "Alright?" "No, I can't see through the windscreen, I'm too small". He returned with some old sacks which I sat on. "There is no engine in this thing" he explained, "but the brakes work, use them if you have to. And keep behind the truck don't wander in or out." As he strode to the tow truck I surveyed my situation. I could only reach the foot brake if I stood up and clung to the steering wheel, and even as I did this the sacks slipped from under me. I released the hand brake and waited. With a roar Revvie took off at his usual top speed, He turned sharp left and up the incline, and how I managed to miss the wall, as I was thrown from my standing position , to slither on the shiny cold leather seat was a mystery. I managed to straighten up as we rushed up the lane with more good fortune than wise judgment. At the top we stopped for a gap in the traffic, and then with a mad dash we shot across the traffic and into the far lane of busy cars and lorries.

I kept squarely behind, but this was the first time I had driven at such a speed and I was so tense that I began to ache all around the back of my neck.

I found my self wondering whether my mother would be able to visit me in hospital. For I felt sure that something dreadful would happen at any moment.

These were the days of trams, and they ran on their set track in the centre of the road. A tram had just stopped and people were just about to get off and on, he should have given way, but not Revvie... straight through the gap. Half standing I held on to the steering wheel, foot poised over the brake, and half shut my eyes. The vehicle seemed so wide I wondered if it would go through.. but it did. We made it! On we drove through the crowded streets, with me hanging on to the wheel, as life depended on it. At long last we were slowing down, we were approaching the multi road junction which was controlled by a policeman on point duty. A quick look in the mirror showed that other vehicles were catching up behind and the policeman was holding his hand up for us to stop. Revvie slowed to a stop and I decided to get up close behind him so that no one would cross and fall over the tow rope and we could leave plenty of room for the vehicles behind. There we sat awaiting the policeman's pleasure. At last there was peace!

The man waved us on, Revvie started forward and I released the hand brake and started to roll backward. For fear of hitting the vehicle behind I applied the brake just at the moment when the tow rope reached its full tightness. The tow rope snapped like cotton. Revvie completely oblivious that we were parting company sailed on at his usual pace. I applied the hand brake and waited events. The traffic to the left moved on beside me, the people behind tooted, gently at first and with growing impatience as time rolled by. The police-man waved me on vigorously. So I decided to get out and explain. I climbed down with great difficulty from my lofty height and approached the constable. I desperately wanted to be friendly so I smiled and said the first thing that came to mind "Nice day!" I was about to launch into an explanation when he turned his back on me and stopped our line of traffic and waived on vehicles from another direction. This squashed any hope I might have had of being popular with the people behind, so I climbed back into my cab to await events.

We seemed to be stuck there for ages before Revvie put in an appearance. He drove straight across, swung round, and backed on. He gave me a look that did not predict well for the future, he tied the rope together with knots, got into the truck and waited the mans pleasure before hauling us back to the garage. He said nothing when we got back, but I was put to helping another man strip an engine down for the rest of the day.

The next day I was again with Revvie. This time we were taking a car out on test. Revvie seemed to just drive with a purpose through streets that I had never seen before. We came to stop outside a house and I was told to sit and wait.

I sat and waited. What else could I do? The car, not fitted with a heater in those days, got colder and colder. Half and hour, three quarters, nearly an hour. I was shivering, freezing cold. Then out he came, got in and drove back at top speed to the garage, telling me all the way things that he hoped would shock me. The full details of how he had been making love to the woman by the fireside. I didn't believe him and thought that this must be his home.

Later I learned from the others that Revvie was married, but that he was carrying on with another woman. Previous trainees working under him had quit because he was always making them wait outside while he visited his fancy woman in the firm's time, any other time her husband would be there.

It was all so sordid, and I had never come across anything like this before. I lost all respect for him, he was a loud mouth dirty minded fellow and I kept as much out of his way as possible, and perhaps the foreman knew how things were, for he often put me with other mechanics.

I enjoyed driving cars, and from time to time got opportunities to do so. I was not so keen on the ingrained dirt that began to soil my hands, or the numerous cuts my soft hands sustained. The romance of the job began to fade. I sought guidance about it and waited. I did not have long to wait. I was asked to put a customer's car tyres up to pressure, and carefully worked the air line, but just as the tyre reached the required level it burst.

I had to report it at once to the office, and the customer came just at that moment. He was angry and demanded a new tyre and inner tube. The boss got angry and demanded my weeks notice.

My motor mechanic days were over. It was not the kind of career I wanted anyway so I left with apologies, and a sigh of relief.

Chapter 8.

It was during one of my many times of job changing that I was offered an office job in London. In fact when I got there the position was filled, but being near the old firm where my brother had worked before he had joined the R.A.F in 1938, I thought it would be nice to call on them to tell them he was safely in India. This was rather important to one of the men there who had served in the army in India years before his retirement.

It was while talking to my brother's ex bosses that I heard of their problem. They just could not get anyone to operate the lift. It was a block of offices at number twelve Holborn Viaduct and their need for a lift attendant to convey all those people to the various floors was vital.

It occurred to me that as I had not got the job I had just travelled to London to obtain I could easily volunteer to take the job to help them out, at least until they might get someone else. In war time London with so many away in the forces, and on essential work there were plenty of job vacancies of one kind or another, but I was looking for something special that would be a God-given future career.

They were very happy with my offer and agreed to keep on looking for someone while I helped them out. So the next day I became a lift attendant.

Of course my friends pulled my leg as to this being a wonderful career, and the "ups and downs" that my life would now experience. Day by day I would catch the train to Holborn Viaduct station and spend the day running office workers and their clients up and down to the various offices. In fact it was rather fun and I met and got to know quite a lot of interesting people. The busy time was when the air raid siren sounded. Then I would hasten to the top floor and start bringing down as many as the lift would hold so that they might make their way to the caves that were under the station beneath us. Some would run down the office stairs, but the top floors needed some assistance for it was quiet a way by stairs for them, especially older people. This procedure happened most days, sometimes more than once a day. Somehow it never occurred to me that I was always the last to leave, and there were times when the raiders would be over head and the guns booming when I started to run to the sheltering caves beneath the station.

The weeks ran by and they could find no one who would take the job of lift attendant permanently. I continued to look out for the kind of work I desired but nothing presented itself, so I stayed on. Then one morning something strange and rather frightening happened.

I was sitting on a small stool in the lift, awaiting a passenger, when quite suddenly I went cold from head to foot. It was as if the blood had drained from me. I experienced what I can only call "a feeling of panic'!

I wanted to rush out of the building, and from that moment onward I had a hatred of that building.

At first I thought I was unwell. I wasn't the fainting kind, but I did feel strange. I continued to work the lift, chat to passengers, and behave as though nothing had happened. But I knew something had happened!

In between lift calls now I spent my time standing on the doorstep or just outside the entrance where I could still hear the lift bell but was not actually in the building. I reasoned with myself that this was stupid, I ordered myself to snap out of it, and made myself go into the building, but at such times I would feel real panic.

This went on for long and almost terrifying days. It was not helped by the difficulties of the homeward journey where a twenty minute trip would now take well over an hour in blacked out trains which moved slowly through the bombing, stopping frequently with long waits.

I now found it difficult to make myself go to work each day, I found myself searching for excuses why I should not go. This was followed by two or three mornings when I really did feel ill, and my mother would telephone the office from the local call box to say that I was ill: But an hour or so later I would feel fine.

I went to see the doctor who called it 'war nerves', and gave me something to steady me down. After a weekend rest when I felt quite fit I decided that I would go to work on Monday no matter how I felt.

Monday dawned and I did feel poorly, but I did arrive for work. It was a tough day to get through with a constant feeling of panic and terror to be in this building, which was only relieved by periods in the air raid shelter.

The journey home was very bad, after an hour the train had only got as far as New Cross Station, and we were ordered out of the train and told that due to an unexploded bomb on the line ahead there would be no further trains. I set out to walk through the blacked out streets of a place I had never been in before, I walked for some time before I found a main road. Three trams were crawling along at a slower than walking pace and all so packed with people, they were even standing on the steps where you get on. There was no possible room for me. A car came toward me, the three slits of the head lamp cover was all I could see but I waved to it.

The window was wound down and I could see that there were six people in a four seater car. The driver was a cheerful old chap and offered to let me ride on the running board until we got a few miles further on where two were going to get out. This was done, with me standing on the car running board and holding on to the top of the door frame.

It was bitterly cold, and I was pleased to be one of three in the back seat after two passengers had alighted. The road home was blocked off at two or three places and we did detours, but in spite of this we made good time and I only had to walk some ten minutes from where the driver dropped me.

That night the bombing was concentrated on our side of London and we got little sleep. When I did doze off I had nightmares which would wake me with a start. My mother let me sleep on, knowing that I had had a rough day, and I awoke after 10 am with daylight streaming through the shelter door.

I hastened to the 'phone box to ring the office, wondering what I would say. I had to wait some time before I could get through and found myself praying "O Dear God, don't let me have to go back to that office."

Suddenly the voice of my employer was announcing himself, I told him who I was and he at once broke into a happy voice "How did you get through? our phone has been out of order all morning. I did not expect you in today, "I know all about your transport problems." "Now listen I wanted to talk to you, I feel rather bad about not being able to find a lift man, and you have been wonderful, everyone in the offices have been saying how well you have done the job. Now listen, what about your own future? We must not be selfish, you have other plans I know."

He went on without me being able to get a word in. "We are happy for you to carry on here but we must think about you, would you like to carry on here or has the time come for you to do what you now need to do for your own future?" He paused and I got in with "Could you manage without me?"

"With difficulty dear boy, with difficulty!" "You've done more than help us out, I get the feeling that this is the time to at least give you the opportunity to stop helping us, what do YOU want to do? come back or call it a day?" I felt sheer joy flowing through me, but I did not want to be rude "If you can manage without me, I.." "Say no more, dear boy, we are indebted to you, and I will put your wages in the post to you".

With a few more compliments, thanks and good wishes for my future the call was over. I felt like dancing all the way home from the call box. I made my way to my room and knelt in prayers of thanks, and even as I did so I did not know what I was so thankful about. I was out of work again and God had not shown me what He wanted me to do.

My pay came by post with a little extra as a thank you gift, and I set out to find a new job, forgetting my experience and irrational terrors. I also lost all feelings of illness.

Something like a week later I was in the City again interviewing for a job when I decided to call around to the old office and see them. After all I had left rather suddenly and they had been kind to me, and I could thank them.

When I came in sight of the office I could hardly believe my eyes. Where 12 Holborn Viaduct had stood was a pile of rubble. I stared at the few men who were working clearing the site. "When did this happen?" I asked one of the men "Not sure" he returned "A few days ago." Then he volunteered something that has lived in my mind ever since. "Bomb went straight down the lift shaft and blew the place to bits! I just cannot describe how I felt. Whether the mans description was factual or not, whether there had been casualties, just why he said what he said I have never found out.

I walked slowly away. I stopped in some doorway further down the road and thought. 'Was it during a daylight raid? Would I have been there? 'I could have been dead at this moment, killed in that bomb incident. I prayed the most sincere prayer of Thanks I had so far known. Perhaps He did have a purpose for my life after all!

I fully admit that in wartime, when so many fellow citizens were killed and injured all the time, it is very easy to feel that someone is protecting you. To have bombs so close that you know they only just missed you. To see houses reduced to a rubble filled bomb crater within a hundred yards of where you are, and this happened more than once, makes you thankful it wasn't you, and feel that someone up there is protecting you.

Perhaps all this is natural, but there were so many times when I felt protected that it felt like blasphemy to think otherwise. I would plan to go somewhere and then not go, only to find out that had I have gone I would have been there when a bomb dropped; maybe killed, injured, or certainly shocked. This did not happen all the time, but often enough to make me believe that God was looking after me, and to be very thankful. about it.

Now many more of my Sundays were spent taking church services as more and more churches heard that I was doing Lay-Preaching, and of course with so many men in the forces there was a shortage of preachers. I was often invited to a little local mission hall, and one Sunday their secretary was telling me how well their Sunday School was going, but that he had a problem. The date of the Sunday School Annual Party was getting near and he had been unable to find an entertainer. Did I know of one?

"What kind of entertainer?" I enquired "Oh a ventriloquist, Puppet Theatre, Marionette show, Conjurer, something like that." he said. I promised that I would try to find someone. However after contacting everyone I could think of I came to the conclusion that there was no one left who could fit the bill. People knew several who used to do that sort of thing but they were not around now. Something had to be done for these children, so I wondered if I could do entertaining. I tried throwing my voice and talking in front of a mirror without moving my lips but it was not so easy as it looked. I spent some time making a puppet and a puppet- theatre but I could never do anything like this in time for the party. I made myself up as a clown, but I did not find it easy to be funny, and there was no one else to work with me for slapstick and custard pie throwing. Finally I was able to buy some books on conjuring, and with my very limited financial resources to buy two professional tricks. I selected a programme of tricks and I practised and practised. When I judged that I might be able to perform before the children I contacted the Mission Secretary. He was still desperate for help so I told him what I had done.

He welcomed my offer with open arms and I went back to practice some more.

My mother found some bits of blackout material and with it made me a jet black cape. But the way the bits came together meant that the seams made a letter 'W' at the back of the cloak. She lined it with some red silk from a dress that had seen glory in the past, and with the bits left over covered up the seam so that I now had a large red 'W' on the back of my wizard's cloak. We thought up the name of 'WIZZ O SO' and so I became 'billed' as 'The Great Wizzoso'. With the catch phrase of "Wizzoso is oh so wizzo". After all if you tell everyone you are great they might think you are!

My first show at the mission party was combined with a bit of cheating, as the secretary hid things about his person and acted surprised at finding the items I had made disappear. But the fact that I had given the children an enjoyable show and that they had not seen through any of my tricks encouraged me greatly.

Within a week I was asked if I would repeat the show for another Sunday School Party, and then another. Within two months I had three shows to my credit, and was known as Wizzoso! The success might have gone to my head, but no one else asked for my wizard performances so I forgot all about it.

Forgot it, that is for a year, when the Mission secretary said that the children had asked for Wizzoso at their party, could I come again. I said yes, and then realised that I would need a completely new performance.

I had noticed that children loved to shout out during a performance things like "It's up your sleeve" or "It's in your other hand". and I had in my last performance traded on this by deliberately getting them to think they knew how a trick was done and, with pretended great reluctance finally showed the other hand.. to be empty. I now worked on this idea for a new performance.

I paid another visit to a magic shop and obtained some chemicals that could 'turn water into wine' although the trick in practice involved my taking some 'wine' into my mouth, and when supposedly drinking from the water glass spitting the wine into it in order to turn the water into wine. The problem being that the chemical in the mouth tasted foul!

I also bought some 'demon flash wool' which is like cotton wool but impregnated with a highly inflammable substance so that when ignited it would make a vivid flash and cloud of smoke (It is often used in pantomime when the fairy appears!) The question now arose how to ignite it?

The answer finally came when I found that old radio valves contained filaments that glowed red hot when a four volt battery was applied to each end, so a few valves were carefully broken to obtain the igniting process. When next preaching at the Mission Hall I looked in at the school hall and noted that the floor boards ran down the hall from the platform where I would be performing, and the floor boards had fairly large gaps in them so that I could run a length of flex from the platform to the back of the hall where I might attach my flash wool.

The day of performance came. While the children were at tea I laid my flex from the stage to the back of the hall and fixed the flash wool. I was hoping to produce a marked ten shilling note at that spot. Just in time the preparations were over and the children rushed in for the entertainment.

I had placed a small strip of metal on the floor of the stage where I was not likely to go, so that when I trod on this metal it would make an electrical contact with a wire on a drawing pin from my battery to the flash wool. Now the Mission Secretary came on to the stage to introduce me.

I hardly heard what he was saying as I was watching his feet getting very near my switch. Finally when I felt sure that he would set off my flash wool I had to walk over to him and gently push him away. He seemed bewildered, so in order to make it seem natural I had to use a trick I planned for later. I put my arm on his shoulder, dived into a small container now in my hand and produced coloured streamers from behind his ear. Happily he finished his welcome at once, took his seat and I started my show.

Most of the tricks I had prepared were home made. I poured water into a beaker, carefully carried it to the front of the platform and suddenly threw it at my audience.. showering them not with water but confetti.

I brought forward one of dad's large flower pots in which I had concealed a spring taken from an old settee. It was held under tension by string and to it was fastened some paper flowers. On top of this I had placed a circular piece of cardboard with a little earth stuck on top.

I proceeded to open a packet of garden seeds, sowed them in my pot of earth, covered all with a colourful cone of cardboard so that none could see the trick work, I waved my magic wand and got my youthful audience to shout "Grow! Grow! Grow!". While the noise was going on the string was cut, the spring threw away the card earth to produced the growing flowers. Looking through the top of the cone with a remark "They have all grown" I made sure that as I removed the cone I took with it the cardboard earth.

Now came the Ten Shilling Note trick. The details of how it was done do not matter here, but I borrowed a ten shilling note from one of the Sunday School Teachers and got three of the children to write down the number and make a mark on it. It was then handed to me and placed straight into an envelope and burned in front of them. I had written 10/- on the back of my hand in soap before hand and I now took the burnt ashes rubbing them on the back of my hand where 10/- stood out in white. "There you are, your ten shillings" I pretended to go on to another trick but of course my audience would not have it. It was at this stage that I suddenly realized that in my preparation I had failed to hide the note near the flash wool. I put my hands into my trousers pockets and sure enough the note was still in one of them. I palmed it as I pulled out the pocket linings to show them empty. "I wonder where it will appear" I called, with more truth than I had wanted. I played around for time but I knew I had to act so I took the plunge. I waved my magic wand and trod on my switch. The flash wool went off at the back of the hall and everyone turned to see. Folding my note as tightly as possible I threw it into the crowd of children. It landed under a chair and happily no one noticed it's passage. "It has returned and it is under someone's chair, everyone look under your chair". There was utter chaos as every child got up and started looking, turning chairs upside down and generally bringing uproar.

Then someone found it. I restored order and had it checked for the right number and mark, and a thankful Teacher had it returned. and the show went on.

Now it seemed that The Great Wizzoso was really wizzo. and I was happy to respond to several Sunday Schools as an entertainer, ever thinking up new tricks, and sometimes buying them. I was fulfilling a wartime need until the 'boys' came home, and making a few children happy when it was most of all needed. But sadly all things come to an end, and so did my days as a conjurer.

One of the Sunday School Teachers worked at the Woolwich Arsenal, a mighty munition making area of which I will say more later. When the childrens Victory parties were to be given he told the works entertainment committee that I was a good conjurer and I was asked to give a performance. I turned it down several times, but they were desperate and pleaded, so I gave in.

The works canteen was an extremely large area with a stage at one end. The children's tea tables were set up longways running from the stage and disappearing into the distance. I prepared on stage with the curtains closed, and after the tea was over someone sang a couple of songs and tried to get the children to join in, but she had little success as most were going to the toilets and moving around. Then I was announced and to be fair the announcer did get them sitting back at the tea tables before the curtain went back. I did my opening trick, but only those near the stage seemed to appreciate it. I lost their attention during the second trick and anyone not watching all of it probably lost the point of the trick anyway. The noise level from the rest of the hall was growing and I switched to my best and most spectacular trick. Only a small group near the stage appreciated it, most of the children who had to keep their head turned to see me anyway, we're just not interested.

I heard a hoarse whisper from behind the curtains "Get him off, he's no good". I bellowed into the microphone system about my next trick, but I could see that they could either not see me or were not interested. I produced a few streamers and fans hoping that the colour would attract, but it was no good. At this point the curtain closed on my act, and also on my work as a not so great Wizzoso! I packed up as quickly as I could while somebody quietened the audience down and introduced another singer. As I packed my final item into the car that my Christian friend had provided, a member of the entertainment committee came over and in silence handed me an envelope. "What's this?" I asked "Your fee". he threw back as he walked away. I ran after him "I don't want money, certainly after failing to please the kids".

He turned and looked at me "That's the fee set by the committee, you've got it, that's the end of it, good night." I could only stare at his retreating back.

Back home my conjuring tricks were packed away never to be used by me again. I refused the one further invitation to entertain a Sunday School, and Later in life I met a man who did a bit of magic and I gave away all my equipment to him. The Great Wizzoso was Dead. The only thing that remained was the cloak my mother had made. This was destined to reappear much later in life when I had children and they wanted to dress up. Then it was used as a kings royal robe, Eastern clothes for various bible characters, and a bridal gown: in black and red? well that's children for you!

The churches were real social centres during the war, and I sang at concerts, acted in plays and helped in events, all to raise money for charities. I joined the West-Bees Concert Party who were putting on entertainment shows.

In one show, as well as my other parts I would constantly appear when the compare was announcing the next item. Dressed in some funny clothes, I would carry a violin case, saying "Now boss ? Now? " His reply was always "No not now" and I would leave the stage.

At the very end of the show the compare would point to a setting sun scenery and say "As the sun sinks in the West" and it didn't, he would repeat it three times. Then I would appear with the violin case.. "Now boss? Now?". He would say" yes all right, Now" and I would take great trouble to slowly open the violin case, take out a child's pop gun and shoot at the sun, which dropped at once. And all the lights go out. "Goodnight".

In one scene the girls would do a beautiful ballet dance to "Artist Life" music, pretending to paint a girl beautifully dressed in a picture frame at the back..

After this we lads would come on in tatty clothes to copy it, we had a lad in the frame as ugly as we could make him, and each of us carried a bucket and six inch wall papering brush. Our attempts to ballet dance always got a laugh! So we tried to keep up the spirits on the home front.

The war, and the day and night bombing continued, and for us in South East London there was no way to forget it or escape from it. If you went to see a film there was always war news, war films, and little notices flashed on the screen to tell the audience that the air raid warning had sounded, that enemy planes were approaching, that bombing was taking place, that the 'all clear' had sounded. To go for a walk was to see bombed buildings, and smell that never to be forgotten bomb-site smell, and join the gas-mask carrying, sober faced people who always looked tired and worried. To stop and talk with anyone was to hear the latest bomb stories, or bereavement news of someone whose man would not return.

Everything was rationed and in short supply, and there was little pleasure unless you made it yourself. The churches were a centre of attraction, not so much for the worship of God but for the comfort to the needy people and the entertainment through dramatic societies and social functions.

I felt both disappointed and relieved when having been called up for the forces I was declared unfit and not required. I wanted to do my bit to defeat Hitler and the Germans but rather thankful that I would not have to rough it in the army. I did, however, did receive a directive that I would be required to do 'war work', and made my way to the Catford Labour Exchange to hear what they would require me to do.

I was directed to work in the Woolwich Arsenal, and duly journeyed there for an interview. Woolwich Arsenal was a city of many miles surrounded by high walls to landward, and the river Thames. It had it's own railway, and transport system, streets, and all that might be needed for the employment of thousands of men and women making everything the army might need.

Each factory was called a 'Shop', and could be located by a letter and number. The 'shops' went on for miles, and depending where your 'shop' was so you entered by a different gate in the wall. Each gate under heavy security. My letter of job application only got me just inside the gate, but I was accepted as a worker, given a pass, and instructed to start on Monday at 6-30 am.

My Father had given up his work to do war work in this same Arsenal. He worked a lathe making something to do with shells for the guns, but he would be working miles away. He did tell me that the journey would take one and a half hours on the tramcar, so I set my clock for 3 A.M. on Monday morning. I had a good breakfast, took my sandwiches from my mother's hand, for she had insisted on rising to see me off, and I walked the mile and a half to the tram stop in the bitterly cold and pitch black morning.

As I had to change trams half-way there were two journeys, and trams are very noisy, dirty, and rocky. They sway about, and if I had not had to change I feel sure that I would have been sick. I finally arrived at gate six and alighted into the dark street. The tram clattered away into the darkness and I shone my torch onto my watch, 'five-forty-five' I was early as usual, very early, I crossed the road to get away from the fourteen foot wall and walked down the road to keep warm.

I came across a cafe, and not only was it open but crowded with workmen. I went in and ordered a mug of tea, and sat on one of the primitive wooden benches, the marble topped table was cold, but the tea was hot and sweet, I sat there watching the men eat bacon sandwiches, and tried not to listen to their conversation where almost every other word was either profane, smutty or a swear word. I had come across bad language before plenty of times but these men had minds like sewers and nothing but filth flowed out from them. I finally made my way to gate six, showed my pass, and found shop C4. I was given my clock card and shown how to clock on by putting it into the time clock and pressing the handle down, and putting the card into the 'in' side rack. I was then seated at a machine and shown how to pull the lever which swung the revolving belt into the drive position which would start things going, and how to do my work there.

Before me was a round metal plate like a gramophone record, with holes in it about every inch; it jerked round in a monotonous rhythm and thump! thump! thump! all day. I was required to pick up handfuls of brass collars from a wooden box with my right hand and heap them onto the jerking plate; my left hand had to move backwards and forwards on the plate so that the pieces of brass fell into the holes. I did not have the satisfaction of seeing what happened round the back of the machine, but the bits of brass were changed in shape and fell out the back into another wooden box. Others were employed to deliver fresh boxes of parts to me and remove the processed pieces conveying them to another machine for the next stage in the production of bullets.

I sat there for what seemed to be all day. Then suddenly a number of bells rang, the machines stopped and I was thankful to think of eating lunch. However it was only ten o clock and I found my way with the crowd to a mobile canteen outside, to buy hot sweet tea and a bun. After ten minutes I was back at the monotonous thump ,thump machine and sat there trying to be thankful that I was at least helping the war effort. If only the machine could go faster I could produce more of these things I reasoned. I asked the man at the next machine if it could be made to go faster. He looked at me as if I were mad "You want to slow down mate or you'll be in trouble". A few days later I asked the supervisor if the machine could be made to go faster. "Are you trying to be funny?" he asked "Or are you just a trouble maker?" I just couldn't understand his attitude, we were trying to increase production for the war effort surely, I felt sure that the machine could be linked to the next size drive which would make it go faster.

The next day two men came to my machine and told me to slow down, I was working too fast. "How can I" I reasoned "The machine is set to go at one speed". "Go and have a smoke in the loo more often" they said. I was flabbergasted! This was sabotage. How would we win the war if we did not go all out? These bullets were needed, I certainly would not go off and waste time in the loo or anywhere else.

As I sat there day after day moving my left hand back and forth and replenishing the pile of brass collars with my right I began to think of other ways of doing this job. I got hold of some cardboard boxes and tore some card into shape, fixing it so that the left hand was no longer needed to sweep the brass collars into the holes, they hit the 'V' piece of cardboard and just dropped in without me touching them.

I next made a cone of cardboard, and with the aid of a broken wooden box I arranged for the brass pieces to fall from the top box, down the cone and onto the plate. I sat there watching it all work for twenty minutes, and all that now had to be done was to occasionally make sure the box was refilled.

If I could do this for one machine perhaps I could do it for others I thought. Just think of the increase in production.

I viewed my work, it was working well, I went off to the men's room. When I returned there was a group of angry men around my machine. They tore down my cardboard invention and put things as they were. I arrived back at the machine at the same time as one of the bosses from the office who demanded to know what was going on "Youngster been playing about, it's all right now" they explained to him.

I started to explain that I had made it possible to work the machine without human attention when one of the men kicked me hard on the shin. "Shut up you fool" he hissed. Soon I was back working my hand on the machine again feeling hurt and completely bewildered. Later one foreman, who seemed kinder than the rest came to explain. If you work too fast on your job the price of the work will be put down and everyone else will have to work faster and for less money. "But" I explained "I can fix that machine so that one man could work two or three machines". "Keep you voice down" he warned in alarm "You wouldn't exactly win a popularity contest now. If you talk like that you'll find yourself lying bruised and bleeding in an alley. You're just a trouble maker, and we don't want trouble here!" I spent the rest of the day just getting on with the job and wondering what all the fuss was about. It just didn't make sense, we were working here to keep our lads supplied with bullets and win the war, any method that would speed up production or get the job done easier and quicker should be welcomed I should think.

When I arrived the next morning I was told to report to the office. I felt pleased, someone must have seen what I did to improve the work, I wondered just what they would say about it. In the office I was simply told that I was transferred to another shop. I found my way there and was given a different job on a machine into which I had to feed bullets into a tray at the end of which a cleaver device picked them up and held them still while an inset was placed inside. Now all day I was picking up handfulls of bullets, flicking them all in one direction and slapping them into the tray. I noticed that if I did not have a break every so often there would be no box of bullets delivered, so I could not but work at their pace most of the time. I sat there thinking of the soldiers using the bullets I helped make. In my mind I heard the call on the battle field "More amo wanted up here" "None left sarg:" came the reply. I knew I must never let that happen. Lives depended on our work, so from time to time I would go and get the next box myself so the I could keep on working, happily no one said anything if they noticed.

Of course I was young and had lived a very sheltered life, with a loving family and a happy loving church people. The factory life seemed strange, sordid and twisted. But I was in for a greater shock yet. The wonderful Holy season of Christmas was drawing near, and I looked forward to celebrating it at work where everyone seemed to be looking forward to it as well.

I was thrilled to see the machine shops decorated with paper chains and coloured balloons and hear the men and women there talking about Christmas parties and celebration. There would be a new and happy spirit in celebrating the Birth of Our Lord. I looked forward to Christmas at work.

At last the celebration day came. We were told that we were to work until lunch time when all machines would be switched off and parties could begin. We were also warned not to clock off until after 4PM or we would loose our pay.

Some show of work was done until the 10 am break time, then all machines were shut off, the noise droned to a halt, and a strange peace fell on the shop. Men and women found boxes to sit on and gathered round in small huddles. Out came beer, and other kinds of drink and they started what they called celebration.

One chap told me to go and get my booze, and twice I was asked to have a drink. When I told them I didn't drink, I was dropped from their 'party', and no body attempted to include me or to talk to me again.

I was shocked to hear the women telling dirty stories as well as the men, and all I wanted to do was get away from what I was hearing. From time to time someone would start to sing or dance about, and I sat among some of them for a while, then I slipped away.

I wandered around looking for a group which was not drinking or with whom I might find friends but I found none. Those whom I had looked to enjoy company with had not come in to work that day it seemed. From one shop to another I wandered hoping to find congenial company, but the picture was more or less the same in each one. In one shop I thought I had found some good entertainment going on where two girls were dancing and everybody clapping in time with the tune, then as I heard the repeated calls of 'take them off' I realised that this was a striptease and the girls had not far to go to complete their act, so I beat a hasty retreat.

I found a magazine and decided to try to find a quiet place where I could sit and read, for there would be a long day ahead of me. There was a pile of boxes and packing cases at the end of my shop so I headed there. As I turned into the area behind boxes someone else had found it first; I don't know who was more shocked, for there was my foreman lying on a heap of straw and paper. His manly chest was being stroked by one of the women, who herself was unclothed from the waist upward. I saw the angry face of the foreman turn in my direction, and the large bare bosoms of the woman and beat a hasty retreat to his "Get out of it you B. *!:!*!".

As I speedily left I was nearly knocked over by one of the young women, a girl not much older than myself. She rushed to the door and flung it open, I wondered what she was doing until I heard her being violently sick outside. I looked at the party going on at the top of the shop. Drink had now well paralysed their brains and most were dancing up and down clinging on to each other shouting "Knees up mother Brown". One woman, usually rather nice I had thought, was laughing hysterically at nothing I could see, I watched her, she fell to the floor and started a new song all by her self "Roll me over in the clover". One of the men went to help her and collapsed on the floor too, they rolled about laughing.

I had seen enough, I had never seen Christmas kept like this, and I never wanted to see it like this again. I went straight for my coat and hurried out of the Arsenal to catch the tram home, with wild thoughts of the big bosoms and what he, a married man was doing with another married woman, of the drunkenness, and all in celebration of Christ's Birth. Perhaps for the first time in my life I thought I knew what the bible meant by the term 'the ungodly'.

I returned after Christmas to find that I had been docked half a day's pay for leaving the smutty party before 4.PM. a price I thought well worth paying. I also discovered that I was once again transferred, this time to work in the office of yet another shop. I sadly formed the opinion at that time that all working class people were like those I had worked with. I found later that many middle class people and upper class too were every bit as bad in their own way. I also later discovered that many working class people are the salt of the earth and that class had little do with being good or bad for there are bad and Godly people in all classes. I was learning!

Chapter 9

Although I was able to hold down the new office work quite satisfactorily in Woolwich Arsenal it soon became obvious to me that I was not doing anything to serve my King and Country there. I was achieving nothing, and undertaking long and difficult journeys daily, under blitz conditions for no good purpose, this all became a good excuse to leave.

When I returned to the Ministry of Labour for a new job I was now classed as a government 'office' worker, so I was offered office work again. This time as a temporary grade three clerk in the Civil Service with The Ministry of Food.

My first job was quite exciting in a way, for I was placed in the Staff Pay department. My task, with others, was to work out the pay of the many staff in their many London offices. I learned to deduct tax, work out increments, and keep a check on sick and other leave. There was travelling allowance and subsistence to calculate, and all in all it was a very demanding job.

The greatest enjoyment however was the paying of the staff on Fridays. The Ministry had departments all over central London, in many different buildings. Each Thursday, with others, I counted thousands of pound notes, putting them, with the silver and coppers into the pay packets, with a statement of the persons pay and deductions. Then on Fridays, I and a senior man, would be driven by a car from the car pool to the various places where staff would queue up for their pay packets. I found it very pleasant to be driven around London by a uniformed woman driver, with our crown emblem marked briefcases full of money.

After a while I was also able to discuss enquiries with these members of staff as to why deductions had been made and how we had worked out their tax deductions.

It was during this time I met some other young civil servants like myself and we formed some good friendships. Eating together midday and enjoying talks, and long discussions.

There was one day, when lunch time came, instead of chatting with these friends I felt that I wanted to be alone, and I made my way to a nearby church for a quiet time. I was surprised to find that another young lad I knew had also had the same idea. We quietly talked together in the church and realised that the other was a Christian, and out of this started the idea between us to endeavour to get others to join us for a quiet time on certain lunch times.

The result of this was the later formation of a Ministry of Food Christian Union which met in that local church vestry, by kind permission of the church vicar. Just how this went on to develop I shall never know, for the Ministry had ways of transferring people and I was transferred to the Audit department. But I left behind me a growing group of ten or twelve people of varying ages and denominations meeting for prayer and bible discussion every week. The Audit department was quite different to staff pay. Under the Auditor I travelled to various food firms to audit their books. I well remember our first assignment, we travelled to a branch of Weddel Cold Store, where I sat in front of large ledgers and called out the amounts appearing in the columns, which the auditor repeated and checked. I had to add up columns of figures and check calculations, inspect receipts and invoices, and generally make sure that the firms accounts were all in order. Practice made me quite good at figures, something I have been thankful for ever since.

As I moved from one department to another within the Ministry it became a real education to meet and work with so many different people. Some seemed full of their own importance, some quite humble. Some were domineering, some were friendly. Some were fun to work with and others almost made life a misery. I did not fully realise it at the time, but I was learning about people, and about life, and it was all vital training for the work I would one day be called to undertake.

By this time I had found out quite a bit about Civil Service procedures and I discovered that I too could put in for a transfer. I requested a transfer to a more local Food Office branch and the transfer was accepted, I became a clerk at the local Food Office in Beckenham, and reported to No.8 Beckenham Road, a large house not far from the centre of Beckenham on the borders of Kent and within easy cycling distance of home.

Here I issued Ration Books to the whole population of Beckenham and learned to answer questions about local food problems, poultry keepers, and the extras for expectant mums.

We had a wonderful staff there at this office and we became like a happy family in that we shared problems, laughed and joked and found each other good company to work with.

The issuing of Ration Books was a major task, and three or four of us would be seated at tables in the hall working hard to attend to the waiting queue. Sometimes one clerk would direct people to which table they should go , and I was always the one to get the awkward or difficult people. For, they said, you are so good at dealing with them. (Flattery got them everywhere)

One day when the queue was extremely long and we were all working just as fast as we could go to clear it, I was working with my head down writing away, when suddenly I glanced up to serve the next member of the public, only to have a very large black trumpet pushed under my nose. My gaze followed it up the long stem, past the right hand that held it, to where it disappeared into an ear completely lost in a mass of grey and black hair.

All I could see of the owner was a nose and glasses on a bed of the grey and black hair, the beard had run riot to his head and the bespectacled eyes were distorted by very thick lens. He looked like some cartoon character or something from outer space. I was completely taken aback, and I suppose my face must have shown it.

From the mass of hair came a crackle of a voice "Ah! What? Speak up young man, I'm deaf you know, what do I do? Ah?"

I looked at the clerk who had directed him to my table and she was doubled up with uncontrollable laughter, tears running down her cheeks. I saw the funny side and I laughed ... right into the old boy's trumpet. He could have been upset, but I quickly joked with him about his trumpet telling him that it frightened the life out of me, and he quickly shared the joke. I showing him special care and help, fitted him up with his ration book and sent him on his way with a smile and thanks for my help. Another satisfied customer! I gained my first experience of what one might call pastoral care when I befriended one of the ladies working in the office. I went to her home to fix her radio set, and there met her husband, her daughter and the grandmother.

It seemed obvious that the daughter was worried and had a problem, and as she was so very attractive it was no trouble to me to befriend her and try to help. Her mother, believing that I would be good for her daughter and could find out what might be wrong, encouraged me to see a great deal of her, so we became great friends.

I discovered that she had two problems, and happily I was able to help her over a very tough time which was only finally solved when she went into the local hospital and had an operation.

That I could be of help to her and the whole family at a time of anxiety, encouraged me to feel that I had something I could give to help others.

I kept in touch with her until she met the man of her choice and I attended their wedding. Although I did not realise it at the time I now think that I learned a lot from this event, and although I have not seen her since I have often thought of her building her home and family in Birmingham where she went to live.

It was June 1944, and Hitler had now started sending over his V.1. weapons, or doodle bugs as we called them. They would fly over with a noise like a motor bike, which was fine if they kept on going, but when the motor stopped the bomb dropped like a stone and blew up on impact.

There was so many coming over every day that we decided at the Food Office that we would ignore them, or we would get no work done at all. The day is vividly etched on my mind when I thought I would be killed by one of them.

While the Food Office customers were dealt with on the ground floor of the old house the main work was done by clerks in the rooms on the floors above.

On this day I had gone to the top of the house to where three clerks were working in the top back room. As I entered the room I could hear this doodle bug roaring away and I looked out of the window to see if I could see it. Yes, I could! "It's coming straight for us" I called to the girls "Let's hope it keeps on then " said one of them. As I watched it coming straight for us I heard the motor cut out. "Down under the table" I shouted in a panic voice "Quick!" I watched it, too fascinated to move. The nose was pointing right at me and coming fast. My blood ran cold and I was rooted to the spot watching it come.

One of the girls saw it as she rushed past the window for the table and she pulled me down, breaking the spell of watching the approaching doom.. I pushed the girls under the table, I threw myself on top of them, and even as I did so there was the loudest, most stunning explosion I had ever heard in my life.

The whole room seemed to jump about and the girls screamed in panic. Masonry, glass, and everything in the room were noisily crashing around us, dirt and rubble were falling all over us, and for one moment I had the impression that the house was falling under me. "Dear God, No!" I cried.

Then as suddenly as it started all was still and quiet. There was a singing noise in my ears as I slowly moved; glass from the window fell from my back where it had been flung. I stayed under the table just long enough to ask if the girls were hurt, apart from glass and dirt in their hair which had made small cuts they were unhurt. I saw that the ceiling had fallen and covered everything, and that dirt and dust was still filling the air like a fog.

I crawled out. I was aware that someone was screaming outside the great hole where once the window had been. I looked out through the hole and saw the smoking crater at the bottom of what had been the garden.

With a filing tray I scraped the broken ceiling from the doorway to get out, and slowly wrenched the door which was partly off it's hinges, from the doorway, enough for us to get through.

Aware that the house might collapse into rubble at any moment, for I could not know the extent of the damage, I cautiously helped the girls across the debris covered landing and down stairs.

Someone was now calling up from below, "Are you all right up there?" Other dazed staff were coming from the other rooms and heading for the stairs.

Happily we were all unhurt though very badly shaken. "Everybody outside through the front entrance" I called, for I had seen buildings collapse suddenly after such extensive damage, and this one had certainly taken a hammering. I was still shaking like a leaf and seeing pin-points of light flashing over my vision, but it seemed important to make contact with the police as soon as possible for the building housed valuable

Ration Books and documents, and the lady in charge was sure to be feeling shaky.

As I descended the front steps with others, a policeman was entering the gate, I went to him, gave his a rather excited report, for I was still in shock, but impressed on him that he must protect the stocks of new Ration Books, which could be stolen. "Leave it to me young sir" he said "But get yourself over to where an ambulance will be very soon, as well for all the staff to get a check up at the hospital"

After standing out front in a dazed condition for some-time they suggested that we all go in the ambulance for a check up, but all I wanted to do was go home, have a bath and rest, so I got my bicycle and went home , to collapsed on the bed exhausted.

I could well remember the first flying bomb we ever saw. As it flew over our house we cheered, thinking that it was a German aircraft all alight. When it was heard to explode we hoped that it had not landed on property. But we soon learned that the flaming tail was the motor that drove it on its path of destruction. Now we knew what devastation and heartbreak they brought.

They came over in droves. Our fighters spent some time trying to tip their wings and turn them back. After this the guns on the coast had a go at shooting them down, and many never reached the populated areas. But our Borough of Lewisham was only four miles by five, yet something over one hundred and fifty of them exploded in the borough, and I still have a newspaper published just after the war which record just where they all exploded in the borough.

Our greatest trial was waiting just around the corner, for when the V2 rockets started falling in September 1944 this was much worse because there was no warning. There were no air raid warnings because no one could detect them. There was no noise for they travelled faster than sound. There was just a very big explosion blowing up whatever it landed upon.

I was cycling along one day when one of these V2 rockets dropped very near. The violent explosion, sound of smashing glass and falling debris, together with the ground jumping about stirred me to action. I turned my bike toward the column of smoke arising from behind the houses, and was soon heading for Pamure Road where several houses had been completely destroyed.

As I approached I was soon unable to ride further for the rubble in the road, so I walked on to see what I could do. A man came staggering toward me holding a very bloodstained handkerchief to his head. I put my arm round him and led him to the kerb, seating him on a piece of wall which was lying there. I reassured him that help would soon arrive and got him to press the wound tight to arrest the bleeding.

A woman came screaming down the road. I ran to meet her, calming her, and holding her. There was blood over her but I could not see from where it was coming. I lead her to sit beside the man. Several people were now walking from the bomb site dazed, bleeding, sobbing. I collected them together urging them to wait together until help came. I moved from one to another doing what little I could, aware now that others were also coming from nearby houses dazed themselves but bringing sheets for bandages and blankets for warmth. All trying to help.

In no time at all there were wardens, rescue teams, fire-men, police, ambulances, all calling orders, and rushing to help. Women from nearby houses started to bring hot sweet tea, I joined in the distribution of it. Someone shouted "Put that cigarette out, No Smoking or lights, there's a broken gas main up there!"

More people were coming from the bomb area now, some helped to walk, some carried on stretchers. There was blood all over most of them. Some were laid on the road to be ban-daged and comforted. I joined my group of wardens and was sent on messages, on visits to other less damaged parts of the roads around to do what I could and report back. Along with everyone else I worked tirelessly to help. A mobile command post was set up, and lists of names of occupants were checked. We needed to know just where everyone was so that we could know just how many were still buried in the rubble.

I suddenly found myself shaking, and realised that I had not eaten for hours. I arranged to go home for food which was eaten quickly before returning. The hours ran on. The rescue teams brought out one after another, some dead some wounded. From time to time now a silence was called, all work stopped and rescue workers listened for tapping or for any sound of life.

On one such occasion the good news came back, "There are two people still alive down there, we have been talking to one of them". All out efforts were made to reach them. Then suddenly there was a "whoosh" and as air was let in, and the whole site went up in flames. Rescue workers had to retire while firemen went in with their equipment. The fire was being fed by gas and it took all their skill and much precious time to get the fire out.

There were no more signs of life! There was nothing else I could do, I returned home for another much needed meal and half hour break. When I returned they were just bringing the last bodies out, there had been no further survivors. The emergency services were packing up and moving off. "We need someone to remain and stay with the bodies until they are collected" I heard the chief warden say. "OK, I will if you want me to" I volunteered "Good lad".

The last vehicle moved off down the hill, and an eerie silence fell over the site. I stood looking at the scene that had seen so much activity. I thought of those I had seen dazed and bleeding, of the hard work put in to rescue, to comfort and help these poor people. Why did God allow Hitler to be born? How could the Germans cause so very much death and destruction, with millions dying and maimed for life in the two world wars they had caused. Would God ever forgive such an wicked nation? I felt anger, and compassion.

As I waited for what seemed ages for the mortuary van, I looked around me. Where once there had been houses with people living normal lives there were now rubble. The typical smell of a bomb site was all around me, damp broken masonry and burnt woodwork, there is no smell quite like it. At long last I heard a van driving up the hill. I waved it down as it arrived. I showed the men where the bodies were, and watched the blanketed stretchers loaded aboard. "Thanks mate, see yer!" they said and the van crunched over the rubble strewn road and down the hill.

I looked at my watch, and as I cycled home I worked out how long it had been since I first ran to help. Twenty-seven and a half hours. I washed and went straight to bed when I got home. Mother was most anxious about me. I slept for over twelve hours and got up feeling poorly and with a headache. A few hours later I returned to my bed and commenced a raging temperature. I heard Mother saying that she was going to call the doctor. I think I said that we could not afford to pay doctor's bills, I'd be alright, but the next thing I knew Dr Richardson was examining me, and prescribing M & B. What ever that was.

Several days later I was getting better, but discovered that I was covered in large red blotches. The doctor did not seem concerned about them and suggested that I might get up. What about these red blotches? What have I got? Is it catching? How long will it be before they are gone?

The doctor looked hard at me, "You are going to have to learn to live with that, they may go soon, or you may have that disease for the rest of your life, it is called Psoriasis, and no it is not contagious".

Little did I realise then, what this life sentence was going to impose on me. For the rest of my life I was going to itch, bleed, and be embarrassed every day. I would never wear shorts or short sleeve shirts again. never have bathing trunks, or expose my body to the sun. And it would impose depression and unhappiness for the rest of my life.

In spite of various treatments, I discovered that like so many diseases, it was incurable as far as the medical profession was concerned. I was told that it was probably brought on by shock, and I would just have to put it down to the war, and blame Hitler. It was also to prove a real test of faith in God. I who had received a blighted childhood through a blood condition would now have to contend with this as well.

Coming near the end of a long and terrifying war I was to face the future with no career or idea of what occupation

I could follow, no educational good standard or examinations to offer an employer, a market flooded with men soon coming back from the Forces and a real limitation on what I could do.

Following discussions with my parents it was decided that I should go to a local college as a day pupil to try to improve my educational standard. With my wider experience of life I was easily top of the class in the content of essays and general knowledge, but in many subjects I was completely ignorant beside those who were just a few years my junior. I suppose I did learn a little, but it soon became obvious that, because of the cost of college fees and the uncertainty of what I was preparing to do, I must leave. It was yet another door which shut.

Following the 'D' day landings and the victories our forces were gaining in Europe, the V1 doodle bugs and V2 Rockets stopped. The air raid sirens ceased to sound, and we were able to move back into the house to live and sleep. Oh those wonderful first weeks of actually sleeping in a bed! After all those years it was like heaven. In May 1945, VE day (Victory in Europe day) came, and we tore down the blackout from the windows and removed the sticky paper from the windows. Although rationing was tougher now than ever, everyone managed to give something for the street parties. In every street tables were set up for the children to eat a victory tea, games were played and in the evening big bonfires lit, the first fires since before the war.

I cycled around from street party to street party to watch the celebrations. The uncontrolled happiness was infectious, people did the silliest things, anything for a laugh! People danced in the street, sang, and went from street to street doing the conga. a popular dance where everyone joins in. People were thankful to be alive, and relieved that there would be no more bombing and destruction.

Although everyone had suffered, most had seen bereavement somewhere in the family and certainly among friends, victory seemed like a safety valve being let loose.

Every church had held special national days of prayer through the war. Now they opened their doors and people quietly slipped in to offer thanks to God for deliverance.

I and a friend opened our Baptist Church Hall, set out as the church. We played very soft background music, and I sat most of one day watching the people come in to sit in prayer and thanksgiving. Some had tears rolling down their cheeks, others looked more happy than people had been seen to be for the weary years that were now mercifully gone.

In August 1945 the two Japanese cities were wiped out with two atom bombs. Although the loss of life was extremely high, it brought Japan to its knees at the beginning of September, thus stopping a war which could have gone on for years with far greater loss of life to both sides. We wondered then, and we still wonder whether it was right to use this bomb, but of course it was not known then whether it would indeed work, nor what the result would be. Like all war and killing through out history, It Is Now History. It is gone! But may we still at least learn from it.

The street parties were once again a feature of celebration, and everyone looked forward to the day when our boys would come home again. Sadly, for so many millions there would never be a loved one coming home. I was now a young man of twenty, and looking forward to what was the Great Day in life in those days, my twenty-first birthday. I would become a man on that day.

I wanted three things for that day. I wanted my brother home from the R.A.F. in India, so we started to pray for that. I wanted a party for all my friends, and for this we would have to start saving up our rations and money. And I wanted a gold signet ring, from my parents; and with a wink my parents said they didn't know, but they would think about that.

I arranged to use the Sydenham Baptist Church Hall for the party on the great day, and worked through out the year obtaining the material and making special fancy hats and decorations.

Perfect in His timing, God brought Reg, my brother home just before the party, and as we shared a bedroom I have happy memories of lying in bed into the small hours talking about all that we had been doing during the war years that had separated us.

I have memories of pushing my bicycle all the way to the hall with a wardrobe drawer across it full with goodies for the party, plus trips with case-fulls. But I got my three wishes fulfilled to perfection. And among my gifts was a still much treasured photo of the air raid wardens, with me in it, and a cheque for twenty-one shillings, with their thanks for all I had done.

The party was a great success, although not without its trouble, for during one game, called Scavenger Hunt, I stood on the stage calling for items to be brought from various teams, one chap named Roy ran up with such speed to get first that he ran straight into me. Some how my knee hit his groin and he was carried from the hall in great pain. Happily he later returned, much to my relief.

My brother, Reg, who had only just returned from a totally different life style in India, and had not yet adjusted to life as he had known it years before, found it all very confusing. His comment after was "Every one rushing about, and bodies being carried out.. I don't know...."

But Reg did have a serious talk with me. "You are twenty one now, and you don't seem to have settled on your future career, The men are starting to return from the Forces, pretty soon it will be difficult for you to get a job." "Don't you know what you want to do?" "Not exactly, Reg, I feel that God has a plan for all of us, and I want to find what His plan is for me". Reg looked at me, there was no getting away from those serious eyes "You must know by now what you can do and what you can't, you must surely have some idea what God wants you to do". The old question was back again.

I opened up to him. "Reg, the only thing I have ever wanted to do was go into the church. When I was Church of England it was to be a vicar. Now I'm Baptist it is to go into the Baptist Ministry. But I don't have anything like the educational standard, and where would I get the money to go to college?". "Am I 'called' anyway?" Reg continued to look at me; Unknown to me, he too had changed from Church of England to Baptist while abroad, now I was hoping that big brother would say something helpful. "Never mind the difficulties" he said "Make an application to Spurgeon's Baptist College and see what happens". My heart felt lighter, I resolved to do just that. I spent some days praying the matter over, and I talked it over with my Minister. There seemed no leading either way, so this time I decided to apply and see where it might lead.

The College processed my application and wrote to me saying that they were happy to consider me as a student subject to seeing me and discussing my application. At first I was thrilled, especially when I showed the letter to the Minister and he told me that there were grants which could possibly see me through college.

Then I went to prayer on the matter. I shared it with my loving Lord, and I wanted to thank Him for this wonderful opportunity. Somehow I could not do it. The longer I spent in prayer on the matter the more I felt that God was not happy with this plan. I wrote to the college telling them just how I felt.

They replied that there was a need for men who would look only to God as I was doing, that there could well be a place for me in college and they would wait to hear from me again.

I prayed! I pleaded with God! I searched through the bible for answers. And then I realised that it was 'Me' wanting to go to this college, and God was saying 'No'. All I was doing was to try to make God say yes to what I wanted to do. As soon as I knew this truth I apologised to The Lord, thanked Him for the answer, and wrote to the college telling them that I could not feel it right to proceed with the application at this time.

A door had been pushed, and although it had opened I had seen that it was the wrong door for me. I was sad, I was back to where I had started. Now God had said 'no', would he soon say yes to some thing? I felt deflated, and not a little depressed.

Chapter 10.

The department store Walter Cobb in Sydenham, where
I had worked as a fourteen year old Display Artist, or
window dresser, had been badly damaged by an Oil Bomb
during the latter days of the war. The centre main part of the
store was gone leaving only a bit each end. No doubt this had
affected business, and out of this came their decision to buy
up an old department store in near by Penge, called Bryce
Grant's.

I had the opportunity to work there now and although I
was employed as a salesman in the china and glass department, the experience was like going back into history.

A small spiral iron staircase in the corner of the store led
up to the floors above. Here were the old living quarters for
the staff of the bygone age when all shop staff lived in.

On the very top floor there was a dark and dingy corridor
with rows of numbered doors. Each door led to a small cubicle
which contained a single iron bedstead, a marble topped wash
stand with jug and basin, a small old-fashioned wardrobe, a
very small two- drawer dressing table on legs, complete with
a looking glass on a wooden stand, and a small cane-bot-

tomed upright chair. The tatty linoleum that covered each floor must have frozen many a dainty foot, and the bare walls bore no sign that any picture had been allowed to break their monotony. The view from each tiny window was largely of chimneys and grey leaded roof.

As I walked through these now forgotten rooms I could picture the shop girls of yesteryear collecting their jug of cold water from the primitive bathroom at the end of the passage, carrying it to their room ready for an early rise in the morning. I could envisage them breaking the ice on a winter morning and pouring it into the basin to wash in an unheated room with the wind whistling through the cracks in the window frame. Being so high up it whistled through now as I looked, and this was a fairly calm day.

I wondered if the girls were allowed to take hot water bottles to their rooms?

On the floor below I could picture the meals being served in the plain dinning room. There were plain scrubbed wooden tables for the shop girls, smaller slightly stained tables for the supervisors, and a polished table for the shop walkers and buyers. Two staff lounges were supplied; I wondered whether one was for men and the other women, or perhaps one for shop workers and the other for higher ranks. Which ever it was they were of poor comfort with their cold polished wooden floors, and wicker and plain upright chairs.

I felt real sympathy with the shop staff of those days, before the Shop Act they would have worked long hours, lived in poor conditions and earned little 'all found'. They would also have been at the beck and call of their 'betters' without redress. I felt very thankful that I had not been born into those days. The ghosts of the past were all around me as I wandered around, and it was not a happy experience.

As I worked in the store as a china, glass, and hardware salesman I was also witness to the transformations that were undertaken by the management. Hoards of workmen moved in to the upper floors to disturb the dust of the past. What were they doing up there banging and bashing about? No one seemed to know at first, then we heard via the grape-vine that a new restaurant was being built, more departments would be there and some offices too. We waited with patience and with duster in constant use.

At long last the rebuilding stopped and the new departments and offices were opened up. But the grandest to my way of thinking was the new "Tudor Restaurant", it was certainly a beautiful place. Old Mr Grant, once the owner of the great departmental store of Penge, now walked the shop floor as a manager. He had seen the store in all its greatness; It was his family store, and filled with memories. He had watched its decline, and now saw his whole life's work altered and modernized.

Had he failed to keep up with the times? Perhaps it had been beyond his financial ability; But now it was out of his hands. Day by day the changes took place, rooms vanished, walls disappeared everything was changing. He said nothing to or in front of any of the staff, but there were times when there were tears in his eyes, and we could all see the heartache through which he was passing. Now he saw the new first floor and the alterations; Whether he did not like what he saw, or was just sorry to see all the old way of life gone, nobody knew: Whatever he felt, he did not stay as long as planned.

Most of the staff said that it broke his heart to see all that he and his family had built up over the past generations just crumble to dust. Whatever the truth, he was no longer seen walking around the store, adjusting this and putting that right, talking to old customers, and signing authorizations. He too, with all the past, was suddenly gone forever.

There was just one other member of staff that remained from the old days. He worked mainly in the hardware department, so I saw more of him than most. At first he fascinated me because I thought he was always having nosebleeds, but I was wrong, he turned out to be the first person I knew that took snuff. He was forever taking a little box from his waistcoat and sniffing up this powder, this caused him to have a running reddish brown liquid from his nose.

I felt sorry for him because he could find nothing to be happy about. He would spend most of the day telling anyone who would listen that the new owners were ruining a good business. Nothing in the world was as good as when he was young, and in his eyes it seemed that no one could do anything right. As he never ceased to moan, he became the target of everyone's teasing, and butt of any bad humour. He was thought of as a miserable old man, and people often got bad tempered whenever he was around, and this spoiled the whole spirit of the store.

He was just as unpleasant to me as to anyone, but I felt sorry for him. He just could not see that he was his own worst enemy. The more he complained and showed bitterness the more he was disliked, and his unhappy life was becoming more unbearable to himself and everyone else every day. As time went on he hardly spoke to anyone on the staff all day. When he did serve a customer it was always someone near his own age, and his attitude was extremely servile, to the customer, sometime embarrassingly so.

After Old Mr Grant left he was called to the office. We were told by staff gossip that the manager was very kind to him and spent some time with him, and that 'he was well taken care of'. But the final link with the store's past was severed, and although some said "Good Riddance", most just felt thankful, or perhaps a little sad. My only other memory of this employment was the day when I was busy serving a customer and I stepped backward into a display of saucepans. The resultant noise and confusion caused the whole store to go silent and gaze in the direction of the hardware department. What made it worse was that the whole display fell onto a lady customer and her little dog. She screamed and dropped the lead of the dog who took off in sheer panic. The orderly decorum of the store was shattered as assistants and customers ran hither and thither trying to catch the yapping little mummy's darling, who thought it such fun to be chased my so many nice playmates.

What does one do in such circumstances? Carry on serving? Pick up the saucepans? Appease the aggrieved customer? Or chase the dog? I decided to appease the one who had received saucepans like confetti. Which turned out to be a wise decision.

The floor walker soon appeared in his neat black suit, rapidly being covered with dog hairs, as he handed over a squeaking wriggling mass, "Your little dog, madam". Within ten minutes everything was back to normal, except perhaps my heart rate and my embarrassment. Later the head of department came to tell me of his displeasure. "Your clumsiness could not have caused more chaos" he remarked. I ought to have kept my mouth shut, but I said "Well of course I'm sorry, but it could have been worse, it might have been that china display over there". I could tell from the look I got that I was not in the business of making friends at that moment!

The next day the offended customer and dog came into the store just to see me. She gave me a little box of sweets, saying that accidents will happen, that she was quite unhurt, and that she hoped that I had not got into any trouble. How kind some people are!

If my job situation was unstable, so also was my social life most of the time. With my membership of the Forsyd Youth Club, my love of modern dancing, and the many young people at the church I was never short of friends. Sometimes we would go around in groups and sometimes we went around in couples. I had a number of girlfriends over the years, some I enjoyed dancing with, some I took out because I liked them, but later as I got to know them I went off them. Some did not like me even though I would like to have taken them out, others showed that they liked me but I did not want to encourage them.

Before I was to meet THE GIRL, there were three girls that I knew at different times and with whom I seriously thought about marriage. The first completely captivated my young heart, we went everywhere, danced, had fun, and worshipped together. When the church wanted a new Pulpit Bible we gave it in our joint names.

We were praying about our future together and seriously thinking of a possible date when we would be officially engaged. Her father loved me like a son and we enjoyed much fellowship together. Her mother slowly showed her disapproval as the relationship grew more serious. I think that her objection was that I had no settled career and therefore was not suitable for her daughter. Oh woman of little faith! Suddenly without reason this wonderful girl broke off our friendship, and I have to confess that at the time it broke my heart. As for the other two, they were not quite so serious, although I did think in both cases that This might be The One! My mind being changed with the last because Miss Right turned up.

The story of my Miss Right goes back really to a request from my church when I was still only around eighteen that I should represent them on the local Council of Churches. During one of these meetings the Council appointed me as the local National Sunday School Union District Visitor. This meant that I visited all the Sunday Schools in the area to help, advise and encourage the work they were doing. I was able to make suggestions of things that I had seen in other schools and in time give advice. But it also meant that I became well know by all the Sunday Schools in the area.

Much later, after the war, some churches had to face changes and one of these changes took place in the Methodist Church. The bringing together of the various strands of Wesleyan and Primitive Methodism meant that one of the local churches became redundant. It was arranged that the church membership would be transferred to the larger Central Church, but nothing was done about the Sunday School work. Those concerned within this church and Sunday School could not see the children turned away, and it was too far to take the children to the central church. With commendable faith they hired the local day school for Sunday afternoons and continued the Sunday School work there.

The Methodist Church had an annual Decision Sunday within their children's work when it was the custom to call the older children to make a decision to commit their lives to Christ, and a special speaker was often called for. Knowing me through my visitation work and as a lay preacher, the Sunday School teachers, when praying about the matter were led to ask me to take this service.

In discussions with the teachers I discovered that there were twelve young people that might respond, and about who the teachers had been praying for a joyous commitment. I duly took the service and as a result eleven of the twelve professed faith in Christ and desired further instruction on the Christian Faith.

In discussions afterward with the teachers it was agreed to start a special club or meeting for these young people, and I was asked to organize it. The result of all this was that every Sunday Evening after the normal service was over, I met together with the young people in the home of a Mr Cox, one of the leaders of the Sunday School. I soon got to know these wonderful young people and although I did not suspect it then, one of them, Audrey, would turn out to be My Miss Right and the future Mrs Gossage.

Audrey was very quiet and said little, she was also ten years younger that I, so I had no thought about her as a girlfriend at that time. Also this was the time when I was serious about girlfriend number one. Audrey, her sister Vera, and the others enjoyed singing choruses around the piano, and discussing Christian issues, doing Bible Quizzes and Crosswords; our Sunday Nights were always very happy times. We also went out and about together as a group.

Audrey's father had died before she was born, and sadly now her mother died. This resulted in the necessity for Audrey to leave High School where she was doing so well, and get a job of work and earn her keep.

It was also a time for me to be led toward work that at last I thought to be a leading where perhaps God was calling: I was introduced to Mr Seccombe, a Christian Managing Director of a firm employing mainly professing Christians. I was invited to visit the firm and have a talk, with him, with the view to my possibly joining them.

Hunt's Agency, I learned, was a very old established employment agency mainly for supplying domestic staff to the nobility, and any one else who were looking for domestic servants; Being in Marylebone, London, it also had clerical agency supplying office staff too. Mr Seccombe was a kindly man who respected my desire to find a life's work and was keen to tell me the great history of the firm, and the hopes for expansion in the future. "We are hoping to open a new branch in Bournemouth" he told me. It is a high class area with a real need for domestic and clerical staff.

"Now that the war is over, we must look to the future, and if this branch is as successful as we think it will be, there may be other areas where we may be able to have branches." The idea of employers having to come to London for first class domestic staff just would not fit into the post-war Britain of the future.

"If you come and join us you will work in each depart-ment in turn and get all the experience you can. Then when we are ready you will move to Bournemouth and manage the new branch". He took me on a tour of the premises. I was amazed to see the masses and masses of drawers in the basement each crammed with details of staff and employers. The building had different departments for each kind of staff. It was all highly efficient, and I warmed to the idea of learning how to deal with each kind of domestic, from butlers to scullery maids. To finding out about the differing needs of the aristocracy, members of parliament, and well known names in society.

"We have great plans for the future". He enthused "And they start soon, for we are at present negotiating for new premises and it will not be long before we move from here I hope". I went home full of what I had seen and heard.

It seemed to me that here was a well established business that I could get into on the ground floor. It was not anywhere near being a Minister in the Church, but perhaps God did not want me to do that, I was not brainy enough for that anyway it seemed.

Now I spent much time praying the matter over. I did not feel that I was being directed into this new work, but neither did I feel that I would be doing wrong to go ahead. I finally accepted, and started in one of the departments dealing with lower orders of domestic life. I quickly learned how to talk to the domestics, sympathising with their experiences and problems but discovering their worth and ability to do the work they had applied for. I also learned how to talk to employers. Not fuss over their requirements unless they wanted to tell you, but from the card information we had to learn just what they wanted, and supply it. I spent time in one department and then moved on to another, and began to be useful in some, but finding others more difficult, having to spend much more time there.

Both employers and employees could be nice or nasty. "Fancy sending me to that crusty old army major, he hasn't a kind bone in his body, he hasn't! I wouldn't work for him if you paid me twice what he offered". Another would call in "Remember me? you recommended me to Lady Woppington Smythe, and I'm so happy there I thought I'd call in to thank you".

An employer might phone "You sent Jones round as a Chauffeur, where ever did you get him from, he's an absolute gem, I have engaged him of course, and thank you so much". The next call might well be "That man Jones you sent round as a Chauffeur. You know you really are slipping up badly round there, you want to watch who you are recommending, this man would be better driving a lorry than a Daimler. Absolutely unsuitable. You must have someone better than that". Strangely what one thought wonderful another would consider quite beyond the pail, and you could never really tell which way it would go.

One Sunday night after our meeting with the young people was over I asked Audrey how she was getting on in the work she had started in a London office. She was polite but I sensed that she was not too happy there. She worked for a press cutting agency, and spent all day cutting pieces out of news papers and pasting them on presentation cards for customers. It did not require much intelligence and she seemed bored, but frightened to entertain any thought of change. I asked her if she would be interested to come and work where I worked? She agreed to my asking if it might be possible.

I fixed things with Mr Seccombe and she got time off to come for an interview. At once he was impressed by her intelligence, manner, and appearance. He congratulated me on finding such a wonderful member of staff, and she started working at Hunt's.

Now each day we caught the train together and journeyed to Baker Street. Train times and my fad for always being in good time meant that we usually had a little time to kill before work, so we started to call in to a nearby coffee house, drink tea or coffee and chat. The distance between us closed as we began to know each other, and admire each other's views and qualities. I think we both began to enjoy going to work and journeying home. I remember thinking "What a pity she is so much younger than I" Ten years seemed such a lot at the time.

Once a month the staff met after work for a time of Christian devotion and prayer. This was not all that unusual in those days, a continuation from what many firms had done before the war. Audrey and I stayed. It felt good to be working among some like minded folk, and certainly was a blessing to those staff who came, but there were one or two who were always too busy to stay.

I was treated as one of the managers, taken out for a meal from time to time and with young Mr Hunt and another manager who operated the clerical agency side, discussed business and other things. At last the move came, and the firm moved to new premises with more space for the departments and a more modern look. This was the step that it had been agreed we should take before stepping out into a branch at Bournemouth. But I felt that my first manager ship was getting near, especially when I was given a Guide to Bournemouth and told what a beautiful place it was.

I began to handle employers as if I were a manager with full responsibility, but there were times when it was difficult to be patient. As I remember it, I had a call one day, and it went something like this:-

"Lady Fotheringay here, you know you really are a very silly man, I understand that you are sending for interview this man Thomas". "Yes, Lady Fotheringay, I think he should be eminently suitable". "Well, I won't see him! You should know, you ought to keep records, I've employed him before, and I had to dismiss him for stealing. It really is too much..." "Excuse me madam,... excuse me .. but madam, this Mr Thomas is not the same Mr Thomas that you employed in 1937". "But of course you'll say that, but I will not see him, you'll have to make up some excuse, and you must pay his fare, it is not fair..." "But madam, the Thomas you employed in 1937 was a much older man if you remember, this is a younger man and totally different". "Is he related?" "There is no connection at all between the man you dismissed before the war and this younger man also named Thomas, he is tall and quiet different". "Does he wear a wig?" "No madam I'm sure this one doesn't". "I don't want to see him, I don't like bald men whether they have a wig or not". "My lady, the Mr Thomas who is going to call on you is a tall much younger man, very well qualified, has never been in your employ before and he is not bald, neither does he need a wig". "Well I don't know". "Madam, I have it on our records that the man you dismissed in 1937 was in his sixties. If you think about it madam, that man must be in his seventies by now and no longer in service. The Mr Thomas you will interview is in his late thirties and a quite different man".

With this, one hoped that the rather bewildered lady would indeed interview the applicant. I would just be getting my coat to go home at the end of the day when the switchboard would say, I have a very urgent call here from a Lady Fotheringay. "Hello! I really don't know what to make of you. That man Thomas, I don't know what you were making all that fuss about, he is nothing like the man I had years ago. Neither was he fat and bald headed. Did you know he has been in Lord Rowley's service for nine years? In spite of you not having a good word to say for him I'm going to employ him. Whatever you say I think he will be very suitable". Click! the phone would be slammed down.

Did I win that one? or did I lose? You can never please some people! On another day one might get a smart chauffeur sit at the desk. You get his file and discover that he had only been a year at his last job. "Why did you leave?" "Well, it was like this, I was cleaning the car in the yard with the hose pipe see, and all sudden like, out came His nibs through the back door, a thing he never does, and he walks right into me hose". "Did he get wet?" "Cor, I'll say he did, soaked.. well not soaked at once, only after he stepped back and fell over 'me bucket of soapy water". "I did try to help him up, but I suppose I ought to have turned the hose off first". "Did you apologise?" "He could n't hear me, he was busy calling me things". At that moment the phone would ring "I say, could you get me a chauffeur rather quickly? I suppose you havn't anyone in your office at the moment?" "Well I might have , can I have a few details sir?" "Sir Guy Ramsey here, Last 'B' fool attacked me with a hose pipe." "No sir, no one suitable for you in the office, but..."

Butlers, Footmen, Valets, Cooks, Nannies, Mother's Helps, Housemaids, Parlour maids, Temporary, Permanents, we dealt with them all; but even as we worked and planned expansion, the world was changing.

The experienced Butler was being replaced by men returning from the war. Footmen were next to impossible to find, and staff were demanding their own sitting room or flat with television and all modern conveniences, also ever higher wages. There was a Labour government, and a new spirit of 'Jack is as good as his master'. The old servant class would never return. Industry beckoned with higher pay and unions, Chauffeurs would prefer to drive for a company, the housemaid and butler moved into the hotel and restaurant trade. The more concerned I became the more I prayed for guidance. I got it when real doubts were expressed that the Bournemouth Branch would ever open. Even the clerical side of the agency looked bad as office staff' agents sprung up all over London, and advertising our services became more and more expensive. Each day I might see our advert in the underground, but there were several others to see as well.

To me the writing was on the wall. I had weighed up this future career but now it was found wanting. Travelling and being with Audrey every day was enjoyable, but I now knew it would soon end. I started to look through the columns of situations vacant in the news papers, there were not so many jobs going now the boys were home from the war, and I did not know what work I should seek. I had done most things, but managing an employment agency was not what employers were looking for as qualifications.

As I reviewed my life at that time it seemed to be in a mess. Beside the employment situation, my social life was of concern to me. I was now too old for youth clubs, and most of the young people I had known had either moved out of my circle through going into the forces, or war work, or they now had differing interests. Some were getting married or working to that end.

I had changed my church, discovering that the Minister at Perry Rise Baptist Church Forest Hill was a wonderful preacher, I had transferred my membership there, so I did not see those of the old church who had known me in previous days.

I had met another girl with whom I was very fond, but now felt very unsure about, so I had kind of burned my boats on that one. One way and another I was not feeling very happy, or secure.

One of the girls with whom we met on the Sunday evenings was Ann, Audrey's friend, and they both came round to my house to listen to records one evening. I had designed and built a new radiogram, and was building a collection of classical records.

When it came time for them to depart I walked them home. We went first to Ann's home and saw her down the lonely lane to the back entrance of her house. As Audrey and I walked back down the lane, we moved slower and slower then came to a stop. I was going to say something, but our hands came together, and we just looked into each other's eyes. Slowly our arms embraced each other and we kissed. Just how long we were there I have no idea, the world seemed to stand still. It was the most wonderful kiss I have ever known, before or since. From that moment on we both knew we would be with each other always. I knew that I had been in love with her for a long time, and that was why I could not feel happy with any other girl. The ten years between us had made me refuse to acknowledge it: But now I knew I loved her. Even if she might one day have a regret, I knew that I would love her always and believed that she would love me. It was a wonderful walk home, I don't think we said much, I don't remember, arms around each other we were too busy floating on clouds. One part of God's perfect will had brought indescribable happiness. We now travelled to work each day arm in arm, and I began to believe that there was something very special somewhere in the future. If I had known that it was still someway off I might not have felt so good, but I now had Audrey to share my future, God had shown me that part of my future, and it was good.

Chapter 11.

I sat down to think things out and review my situation. What did I want to happen? What was going to be my future? I would want to get married and settle down, and for this, stability was essential. I had spent years looking for some special work where I could serve God and my fellow men, as far as I could see I was no nearer now than I had been when I left school at fourteen. I was now ready to admit that this way was not paying off, it was no future to offer Audrey. Whether I had been right or wrong about the past efforts to find the right career it now no longer mattered, I was now in my late twenties and I must find a secure job and settle down. I prayed for work that would offer security and money so that I could prepare for a future with Audrey.

The answer came almost at once with an advert in the local paper for a service engineer. As I explored what the employer offered it seemed tailor made for me. A large company which would train me in their own training school. If I passed their exams I would be supplied with the tools to do the job, and would go round servicing their equipment. There was only one snag. I would have to supply my own car. I told them that although I did not have a car, I would get one. The thought of becoming a car owner was a great attraction for me.

The firm was one of the leading manufacturers of vacuum cleaners, and my job would be to visit customers' homes and service their equipment. The company did things in style. I was lodged in a hotel for the period of the training course, not that I saw much of the hotel as I had so much home work to do after each day's training.

I started the course with about twenty other men. I now learned that there were three kinds of dirt. Fluff, Dust, and "dangerously destructive, deeply embedded, germ laden grit". We learned all about carpets, the different types, how and where they were made, and I was supplied with a book on carpets, the different types and how to recognise them. We studied the construction of other floor coverings, and we all worked hard and helped each other understand and remember all the things we were learning.

We were given the history of house cleaning, the earliest forms of the mechanical cleaner, the principle of other vacuum cleaners and the difference between our company's and the rival companies. We were made to demonstrate our cleaner against every other make, and we all ended up completely sold on the idea that ours was the best.

After lectures on our product and how it worked, We turned to the practical. Each of us was supplied with a metal tool case, complete with a mega to test electrical safety, and all the screwdrivers and tools we would require, including a grease gun with the special nipples to fit the products grease points.

We had to learn the model number of every model that the company had ever brought out, and learn the correct procedure on stripping, cleaning and servicing it, and of replacing parts. We practised and practised, answered questions fired to us at random, until we felt that we could do it all almost blindfolded.

A small ring binder was supplied, and as each section of the course was passed there were new sections of information supplied for the ring binder. Now came a detailed list of all parts and the ordering numbers. .Also the forms we would have to use.

The next part was introduced with great care. There were, we were told, large numbers of our old model cleaners still in use, a tribute to the great product the company produced, but they would not last forever. Also some housewives liked to replace their equipment for the latest and best. We were now to learn how to demonstrate and sell customers our latest product. There followed a sales course with patter that left nothing to chance.

They asked, Was there anyone of us there who would turn down the opportunity of making a little extra money if it came our way? We would get commission from the local dealer whenever we sold a new machine for him. The sales course was very thorough, practicing objections to buying, hire purchase, and what to say at each and every turn of the selling. Our ring binders were now full.

The course was now into it's second week. I asked the main lecturer if he thought I would pass their exam and be employed, as I could not afford to buy a car if I was not. He assured me that I would be accepted, so I called on the local car dealer where I had been eyeing a car that I wanted, and settled on buying my very first car. It was very old, a 1934 Austin ten. It looked a little like a London taxi with it's square features. It cost £110.00 a great deal of money in those days, and of course it officially belonged to the finance company with whom I had a hire purchase agreement.

I remember driving it into the hotel forecourt with pride. I also remember I was so excited that I awoke very early the next morning just to look out the hotel window to see MY CAR standing there. I remember it's registration AYX 765. and it had that lovely leather smell that old cars had, now sadly lost by the introduction of plastic.

The oral and written examinations took place and were as frightening as all exams. The questioning attitude as to how we had done after it was over was the usual nightmare. We waited for the results. All but one of us passed, and I was allocated to the Bromley and Beckenham area and instructed to meet the supervisor on Monday morning in a local cafe.

Monday came. My car parked in the road, my new tool case waiting inside, I met the supervisor, with ten or a dozen other men, and was given a set of cards on which was recorded customers names, addresses, and details of the machines that they possessed. My task was to service a set number of machines every week, to arrange demonstrations of new models, to demonstrate them in the evening when hubby was at home, and to sell new cleaners. I enjoyed the servicing, found it difficult to arrange demonstrations, harder to demonstrate, and extremely hard to sell.

From time to time the supervisor would come with us and show us how to do it. He certainly knew his job, and he certainly sold new cleaners. Together with the few I did sell I found myself winning small prizes. A pair of cuff links, a pewter mug, and so on; but a full day's work and most evenings out demonstrating and selling made a mess of my social life, and it was a wonder that Audrey put up with my excuses for not taking her out.

We became engaged, and started to plan for our future. The biggest problem was where we might live. So many homes had been destroyed and still not rebuilt, also with men home and settling down there were very few flats and no houses to let. We did consider buying, but all we could find at our price were much dilapidated places which would require either a great deal of money or a D.I.Y buff who had much time to put it right. Neither was therefore for us.

It was into this desperate situation that an Aunt and Uncle of mine came. They lived in a luxury residential caravan. "Live in a caravan" they advised. We explored the situation and the more we looked at it the better it became. Having prayed for guidance we visited a caravan dealer and looked over his stock. There was one which we liked more that all others; The salesman dealt with our objections one by one. We could afford it on a hire purchase agreement, and when it was paid for we would only have to pay the site rent.

But where do you put a caravan somewhere near my work in Bromley? He had the answer for this too. If we bought the caravan from him he would get me onto a site in Biggin Hill, within reasonable driving distance of Bromley. We went and looked at the site and it was acceptable at ten shillings a week rent. We looked at the caravan we loved, and signed up. The wedding day was set 20th June 1953, and the date of delivery of the caravan to the site was the morning of the 2nd of June. All was going well, and we were excited.

Audrey and I arrived at the Caravan site in Berrys Green, Biggin Hill in good time for the delivery. Apart from the house where the site owner lived there was a community meeting lounge, and we spent our time between watching the Queen's Coronation on a television they had hired for the caravan dwellers and looking for the arrival of our future home.

Hours late our Bluebird Challenger caravan arrived. We had chosen a pitch at the very top of the field, which sloped downward. A few kind friends from other caravans helped us place it in position, and in no time at all we were putting a few personal bits in and having our first cup of tea in what was to be our new home, after the wedding.

The wedding itself had a problem for me. Audrey would be nineteen, under the age for marriage without parental or guardian consent. Audrey had no parents living, and a step brother had not wanted me to marry Audrey, and had said that the wedding would never take place. As he was very ill and weak I did not want to argue or tax his strength, so I now made arrangements to ensure that Audrey could marry without anyone's consent, that meant that no one spoiled Audrey's wedding day.

The Minister at Perry Rise Baptist Church was kind and understanding as well as being such a great preacher, and together we arranged everything so that all would go smoothly, also, as we felt that God had something special for our lives in the future days, we had included in the service a special place where we dedicated our lives to Our Lord.

I was pleased that not only Audrey's brother and two sisters would be at the wedding, but both step brothers too, one travelling quite a distance and bringing his daughter to be a bridesmaid. I paid a courtesy call on them the night before the wedding. "I suppose that you want one of us to sign some papers giving our permission" said one. "No" said I "for Audrey and I it is just very good that you will be there to wish us well, we shall need nothing in the way of signatures, just enjoy the day with us". They had obviously been discussing the matter and now seemed deflated; but it was good to have them there.

One of the chauffeurs I had known from Hunt's Agency days, Sid Mace, lived near us, he, and his lovely wife and daughter had become dear friends. Learning of our coming wedding he had gained special permission to use the Rolls from his employer, he was to drive the bridesmaids and Audrey to the church by 10.30am, and see some others home after. Reg, my best man, and I travelled to the church in my Austin ten, leaving it ready for a quick get away afterwards to our caravan.

I felt no nervousness at all, perhaps because I was used to taking services and preaching most Sundays. Audrey looked stunningly beautiful in her white gown, with a bouquet of red roses. All went well until the prayer, when I was aware that something was going on just behind me. It appears that one of the bridesmaids fainted, and had to be supported by her father and uncle. The feeling of joy and God's presence was uplifting through the service, it was truly a great day.

We had arranged for a buffet lunch to be laid on in the church hall after, but we had made one mistake, The photographer had persuaded us that he could return within the hour with our proofs and take orders and we had agreed. Now it was a question of all ceremonies and food over but we were waiting about for the photos. Sid Mace had excused himself to leave after the service, promising to return in good time for our departure. He had not returned, and we wondered where he had got to. We later learned that he had parked the Rolls on the hill outside his house while he popped in for just a minute, and a beer lorry and trailer had driven past up the hill. The trailer had broken loose and rolled back smashing into the Rolls doing massive damage.

Audrey and I finally departed from the church in the little Austin, it all must have been a success, and I found confetti in that car constantly right up to the day I sold it.

Sadly we could not afford a honeymoon, but we did have our new home to go to, and our caravan became our honeymoon home. I have always regretted that I could not give Audrey a proper holiday honeymoon, and have frankly been a little envious of all the couples I have since married as a minister who leave for some romantic honeymoon, but it is past and gone now so that ends the matter. The caravan was an ideal way to live. Centrally heated in winter, and like a holiday in summer. We learned to be tidy, for you cannot leave things about in a caravan or it soon looks like a tip, and nothing can be found when you want it. There has to be a place for everything too or things get put where you cannot remember where they are. Audrey one day made a large batch of cakes, too many to get into the cake tin. She put the remainder in the flour tin to keep them fresh, this being a spare tin anyway. They were found some time later.. very much gone off!

I was now getting nicely settled into married life, we attended Biggin Hill Baptist Church and joined. Driving from Biggin Hill to Bromley every day, I would do my service work, book what demonstrations I could, call back in the evening and sell if possible.

The supervisor now called us 'sales men', not service engineers. And I got the impression that I could never sell enough to please. He told me that the company were not satisfied with my selling record and that he was going to come out with me to help me. He looked through my cards and pointed out a customer with an old machine that was about due for service. I did the service while he was pleasant to the customer. Then, just as I was about to reassemble the machine he stopped me. "Look" he showed me "Just let the screwdriver cut in here like this. Now run it and see what happens". I switched on and the small blue sparks around the comutator had turned to a flame. I was about to say "look what you have done" When he called the customer over "Look at this" he invited. He switched on and she saw the flame. "I'm afraid this could never pass our safety test, this is dangerous!" "Oh dear" she said "What does that mean?" "It means that your armature has gone, how old is it?" She told him. "Well it HAS done well, we don't see many of this model these days, we stopped making these a good many years ago". She looked at him anxiously "Can you repair it?". "You can't repair armatures, and I doubt if we would have any old ones of this model from which we could take the armature and change it". He paused in thought. "I have an idea" he said. He went out to his car.

In no time he was back with a brand new boxed cleaner. "Could I borrow a knife to open this box?" Soon he had the lady helping him to set up the new cleaner. I'll take yours and see if I can do anything to help you out, and so that you are not left without one, use this, it's our latest model. He showed her how to work it and got her to start cleaning with it. "We will be back tonight, let's hope we can do something for you".

We moved on to the next service job. I was struck dumb, I just could not believe what I was seeing. Later that evening we returned with the old cleaner which had been in the back of his car since he threw it there. He explained to the husband what he had told the lady earlier. "The spares for this model were used up a long time ago, and I cannot help you at all" he lied. "Did the new one work alright?" It had. "Well it would, it is so much more powerful than your old one". Within twenty minutes he had the hire-purchase agreement signed, having knocked two pounds off the deposit if he took the old one away. (There may be bits on it I can help someone else out with). We went on to the next evening call and sold another. We sold eight new machines that week, mostly by cheating and lying; and the old machines would be sent back to be reconditioned and sold as such. With commission on the new cleaners and something paid on the old ones I did very well that week, but at what a price.

I made up my mind that I would never lie and cheat in this way, It was wrong. It was also certain that the company would not agree to such practice.

Then the company went into the Washing Machine market. We went on a course to learn all about them, how to service them and how to demonstrate them. We learned to demonstrate doing a normal wash within an hour and wearing our good suit without getting a spot of water on ourselves or the floor. Washing must look quick and easy. We were taught how to sell them.

I called into the dealer to take a washing machine, but I could not get it in my Austin, the door space was slightly too small. I asked the supervisor what I could do. "Simple" was the reply "Buy another car!" I gulped at the mere idea "I can't it is on hire purchase". "No such thing as can't, the condition of your employment is that you supply a car". Although I argued, that was as far as I got.

I started looking for another car armed with a tape measure. I found a sleek grey Triumph Dolomite, and with much sorting out with the dealer I was able to cancel one agreement on the Austin and start a new one on the Triumph. The change over was made, at a price! I now did as much as three or four family washes in a morning and began to sell them fairly well. They were excellent at getting clothes clean, easy to use, well made, and few people had washing machines so there was a market waiting to be tapped.

Our little Baptist Church was getting excited during these days. An American Evangelist was coming to this country called Billy Graham. We arranged to go by coach to hear him. I had never seen a Christian meeting like this one. Harringay was packed.

I heard his message and was impressed although I did not like his American accent, and manner. I did not go forward at his invitation for I had already committee my life to Christ. However there was something he said that bothered me.

I was concerned by the phrase "You either give your all or nothing at all'. What was ALL'?. Day after day I now wrestled with this. I came to believe that I had never really given my 'all'. Would I give up Audrey? My Mother? My car? Would I be prepared to go off to some Bongo Bongo Island as a missionary? Would I accept a life of complete poverty, for the rest of my life? The answer seemed to be 'no'. Were there areas in my life where God did not have a place? I felt that there were.

Even as I realised the truth of this I seemed to feel God slipping away from me. Sunday, which has always been the happiest most joyous day of the week, this week seemed dull and uninteresting. After a few more days of constantly questioning and arguing with myself in every waking moment I could stand it no longer. I must settle this one way or another.

I left the caravan, walked down the field, I walked and walked, thinking and thinking. I was now standing in some woods. There was no one around, all was quiet. I resolved to either turn and walk back saying 'I come first' OR I would tell God that He came first. The battle within me raged and it seemed as if all nature held it's breath. Then I knelt down on the carpet of leaves and spoke to God. I told Him that I now gave myself to Him completely and without reserve. If He wanted me in some outlying place as a lonely missionary I would go. If He wanted to take away everything I had He should do so. All that I was and had was His, now and forever.

I remember adding that I hoped that He did not take everything but if He did I would accept it. I was His to do with as He chose. I returned to the caravan as one who has lost a heavy burden. I felt happy and free, and like someone in love.

I did not know it but God was going to take me at my word. He was going to knock me down to the lowest, before He started to build me up.

The first thing that happened was to do with the car. It was now unreliable, always having something go wrong.

I spent money to have one thing fixed and something else would go wrong. I kept telling myself, 'If I have this done it will be OK'. It wasn't. Again and again I told myself that if I just have this job done what else could go wrong; but there always was something else.

My customer servicing started to get behind, I missed appointments, I was late in the morning because the car would not start. The supervisor carried me for a bit, then clamped down. If you cannot supply reliable transport you cannot do your work properly. If you cannot do your work properly you will have to leave the company. Almost at once the car broke down again and went in to the garage for three days. When I collected it I was out of work.

I had to do something quick, car repairs had taken any savings that I had. I answered an advertisement to be a representative of a small unknown little company, selling an obscure make of vacuum cleaner. Their system was to advertise in newspapers and invite members of the public to have a demonstration of their cleaner. I was given a very large area, and any replies within my area was sent to me and I had to go and demonstrate and sell. The adverts came from all over, and I started clocking up hundreds of miles a week. I did sell quite a few, and they were a good, well made cleaner. But the car started to complain and there was a repeated performance of no car, no sales, no job. I was out of work again !

The Ravensbourne Car Hire Co were advertising for a chauffeur, I applied, and was taken on. I arrived for my first morning and was told that I only just had time to get to my first client, and I was to take the Buick standing outside. Trying to work out how to get to the address as I went. I got into the drivers seat, but I just could not find the Starter. I hunted for a button on the floor, the dashboard, the steering column, everywhere ! I finally had to go and ask the boss where it was. "It's got an accelerator, just put your foot to the floor on that". I switched on, pressed that peddle to the floor and I was away . Most of that morning I was told to go here, there, and wait, while they did shopping and other calls.

Later on I discovered that the client was a relation of the boss, and they just wanted to see how I performed. I must have satisfied them as I was accepted as a chauffeur, peak cap, and all!

Only a few days later I was called into the office and sacked. I asked why, and was told that I had over charged a customer the previous night. Up to this point I had been a little in awe of the boss, but now I was angry and raised my voice "This is grossly unfair" I told him. "I am new to this job and have done my best to use your night time charges. Everyone is entitled to make one mistake, you are being unfair".

To my amazement he backed down, said I was right, and that he was sorry. "Try to get it right in future" he smiled.

The following Saturday I was given an all day job to take a family some way into the country for a wedding, it was one of those days when everything went just right. The weather was perfect, traffic good, and I arrived perfectly on time.

I was given lunch and made to feel like one of the family, I drove them, and some others to the church, I watched the wedding from the church gallery, and drove several car loads to the reception after; where I was given a table all to myself.

When the speeches were all over they wanted to dance, and they asked if anyone could play the piano, It seemed that

I was the only one who could, so I played waltzes, quicksteps, foxtrots, and tangos, and a happy time was had until it was time to drive my party back home.

As I held the car door open for them to alight they were full of thanks and praise for "making their day", and they also showed it by a handsome tip.

I had made it plain that I did not want to work on Sundays, but a week later I was ordered to do so. I had never worked on a Sunday before and it turned out to be the most miserable day of my life. I only had two small jobs all day, and stood watching people attending morning and evening church, and wished I could enjoy joining them. I got fed up with reading, and there was nothing else to do all day.

When I was asked to do this Sunday Duty every week, I said "No". The boss being in a bad mood sacked me, and that was the end of my chauffeuring.

I was desperate for a job. I took the only one that offered. I caught the train to London to spend each day trying to sell carbon paper. London is full of offices, offices are full of staff who will not let you see the buyer. Offices are also full of cupboards that are full of carbon paper.

For ten days I tramped the streets of London, up and down stairs, in and out endless doors trying every method I knew, to try to sell carbon paper. I had not obtained one single order. Finally I entered an office. The young lady, it's only occupant, smiled at me, and said "You poor man you look worn out come and sit down before you fall down". I sat obediently. "Just you wait there" she smiled. I was happy to rest my weary bones.

She returned with a cup of tea, and a remark that amazed me "You are a Christian, aren't you?" "Yes, how do you know?" "The Lord has His ways" she grinned. "Now what are you selling and how is business?" I told her I was trying to sell carbon paper and had yet to make my first customer in ten days. "I will take one box". I readily got out my unused order pad and wrote. She signed the order, and walked to a cupboard which showed that the office already had a full stock and it was not really needed. "They have left me in charge and given me a free hand so it will be all right". she assured me "it will all get used".

As I drained my second cup of tea we exchanged information about our churches. Then she said "Let's have a prayer then before you go." She proceeded to pray as if she had known me all my life. Thanking The Lord that my ten days of trial were over and asking for grace that I should remain faithful, as His wonderful will now started to unfold to me. A handshake and I left with a light foot.

I went home and slept soundly that night. The morning post brought me a letter from the carbon company saying that as they had received no orders from me they did not think that I should continue. There was a very small cheque enclosed to cover expenses incurred, and it did little more than that. I talked over our situation with Audrey, and we agreed that we should consider leaving our caravan home which soon we would not be able to pay for, and see if we could live in with my parents until I should get settled.

I felt heartbroken to let Audrey down like this, I was the provider, I should at least be able to keep her in the style to which she was accustomed.

With my parents agreement, we placed an advert in the paper to sell the caravan. Almost at once a lady applied, and agreed to have it for the cost of the hire purchase we yet had to pay. I still have her lovely letter thanking us for leaving the caravan in such a clean and polished condition, and enclosing the official acknowledgement that the finance company had now received it's due. We moved to Sydenham, having one room and sharing the kitchen with my parents. I advertised the car for sale and found a buyer at once. I gave him the honest history of the car and all the bills that I had paid putting it in good condition, so that he would know what had been done. He came and collected it and drove it about for a week. Then on the following Monday morning as he was going round a bend in Catford the steering locked up tight so that he could not move the steering wheel. It crashed into a wall happily without anyone being injured, I think that the story ended up with the car in the scrap yard. The man came to tell me about it, assuring me that he attached no blame to me. I had been honest with him, but that it had not been an entire loss for he had received some compensation from the insurance company. A neighbour passed the comment "Some one must be watching over you, you could have been killed in that car". It certainly made me think that we had a God who was looking after us, and must have some other purpose for me.

There was no time for picking and choosing work now, I just placed myself in God's hands and went for the first job I could get. This turned out to be a 'Tally man', as the trade called it. I was attached to a large department store connected with

Great Universal Stores. My job was to visit customers each week to collect money for goods that they had purchased, and to persuade them to buy more. I carried catalogues, which were left with customers, and I would from time to time introduce new items and bargain offers. Women's and children's clothing was the most popular, followed by menswear and household goods. I bought an old car to get me round and carry the goods. In my daily calls I rarely saw the men folk, almost all buying was done by housewives.

Some women had no idea of how to budget and would buy far more than they could afford, this made for discord between husbands and wives and the poor tallyman was often in the middle. "Don't sell my wife anything else", a husband might say. But the wives would plead "How am I going to clothe the kids if I don't get things from you and pay off each week"? Some women who could not pay would be 'out' when I called, and this meant going back at various times to catch them 'in'.

Some of the other Tally men found temptation in visiting the women. One man came to me to ask for advice on what he should do. It appears that he sold a housewife some underclothes and offered to go into the bedroom to make sure that they fitted. Now she was expecting his child and her husband was returning from his work which had kept him absent for many weeks. That particular story ended with the husband finding out and putting the man in hospital after a fight. He was sacked and when I last saw him he was out of work and awaiting a court case. Nothing was said about the poor woman and the family he had damaged.

I was well liked by my customers and as they got to know me I became a friend and confidant. I solved many a problem, and handed out much advise which was successfully followed. I began to feel that I was doing something helpful although I disliked encouraging people to 'live on tick'. If they had only saved up their money they could have had the pleasure of going to any shop to choose their goods, would have paid less for it, and in their financial condition, that would have helped them, for every penny counts when you are poor. The firm now insisted that I take an additional area which was a very poor district and had much outstanding debt. I was told that I must collect these debts in. The previous man was now too well known and the debtors knew his face and would never open the door to him. This meant that I had to spend all my spare time trying to catch these people in and make them pay. Sometimes to catch the men coming home or going to the pub when they might have money on them. Life for me became more difficult and miserable.

Chapter 12.

Just one year after our wedding we were back in Sydenham living with my parents, and we knew that come July or August we would have our first child. We therefore made the decision that instead of journeying to the Baptist Church Forest Hill, where we had married and had friends, we would start attending the Congregational Church in Jews Walk, which was just at the end of the road. We reasoned that it would be so much easier for Audrey both before and after the baby was born. We now found a new set of wonderful friends. we joined whole heartedly in all the activities, joined the choir, and enjoyed the ministry of the Minister, Rev R.W.Carr.

We were joyously received into the Church Membership, and I attended on Sundays whenever I was not out preaching elsewhere. On several occasions I conducted worship and preached there when the Minister was not available.

In the early hours of Sunday 1st August Audrey was rushed off to have the baby. I was told that I could phone after nine so I went back to bed; but at one minute past nine I was on that phone and was told to "please wait". After just a few minutes,

I was informed that we had a daughter. Barbara Christine had arrived and I told everyone I could think of before going off to take a service myself.

Life was tough as far as my work was concerned but now I had to work harder and try to build us a home. I bought various items of furniture from time to time and we had our name down on the very very long housing list. Money was always short, and that winter I had been very happy to have the gift of an overcoat.

God had certainly taken me at my word and taken most things away. Home, car, money, and everything we could turn into cash. From now on the building up was very slow. But I had Audrey and now little baby Barbara. I wondered sometimes if I might get a call to a Bongo Bongo Island any day!!

The new pattern of Sunday life was that we attended church together in the morning and I went alone in the evening. Unless I was out preaching. One Sunday evening the service had closed and I was chatting to friends when the Minister came over and said "Don't go yet, I would like to see you in my vestry". I thought that he would want me to tackle some task in the church, so I turned up in his vestry.

He sat me in a comfortable chair and looked straight into my face. "Why aren't you in The Ministry?" he asked. I was taken aback, and paused before I answered "I did feel that I was called once, I even applied to the Baptist College, and they were happy to consider me, but I became convinced that God was saying 'no'".

I got ready to go. But the Reverend Bob Carr had not finished with me yet. "Why aren't you applying for the Ministry now?". "God does not want ME, beside I am married now with a baby, I could not go to college now. It's all too late". I said regretfully "How do you know that God doesn't want you? He is telling me that He does". This shook me! I did not know what to say to that. "Tell me" he looked me in the eye "Which is more important to you, Doing what God says, or the difficulties that stand in the way?" I was able to look straight back "I have told The Lord clearly and plainly that I am completely His to do with as He wishes, now or at any time. He knows that He has only to convince me that He wants anything of me and I will respond. I am about as far from the ministry as it would be possible to be I should think".

He sat back with a smile. "Tell me about the difficulties". "Do you want me to list them?" "Yes, go on, do that". I paused to collect my thoughts "When I left school at fourteen I was about at the bottom of the class, I am now thirty. I could never get through college. Then, I am just about flat broke, I have no money to go to college. I have a wife and baby to keep, what would happen to them while I went off to college?"

He leaned forward "And now see what might be on the positive side. You are an able preacher of some fifteen years experience. You are good at dealing with people. You have a wide experience of the church, it's work, Sunday School, and youth work. You are a faithful member of Christ's Church and a very good influence on other people. If you were prepared to work hard you could go into the Ministry without going to college through our 'List B system', and God Himself would deal with all that you lack if you trusted Him".

It was my turn to question now "Do you think I should go for the Ministry, or do you KNOW that I should?" "I know, but that is not important, what matters is that YOU should know, what do you think God has been doing since you left school but give you a vast experience, and test your willingness to serve Him ?". That I had not thought about!

"I'm sorry" I responded, "But I will do nothing unless God convinces me".

"Then He Will convince you" his voice was quiet and relaxed, "But tell me, what is the one thing that would stop you from taking the first step and studying"? "Well that's easy" I grinned "I would need to have time to study. At the moment I am 'bad debt collecting' and it takes all the hours that I have, and I hate it". "Then will you do this one thing I ask of you, will you Pray about getting a new job; And start looking for one"? I smiled a reply "All right, I will". We prayed together for a while and I returned home to tell Audrey. I decided to pray first. If The Lord wanted me in the Ministry it was the biggest thing in my life and I had to be absolutely convinced that it was His idea, not mine. I spent the week praying at every odd minute that I could. The only impression I got was a feeling that my Lord was very near and that He was smiling at me, as if He knew something that I did not, or a 'just you wait' attitude.

I found it nice but puzzling, and rather thought that I was perhaps kidding myself because I wanted some response.

On Friday my Mother brought in the local newspaper which she took regularly, I was up early and had time to look at it over breakfast. Remembering my promise to look for a job I turned to the situations vacant columns.

At once my eye was taken to one advert half way through a column, it seemed to be in very dark special print, so I read this first. It was for engineers to service equipment in the local area. Training would be given, apply Ascot Gas Water Heating Company. I looked at my watch, just gone eight-thirty, I would ring them straight away. To my surprise I put the phone down having made an appointment to see them.

At the interview I discovered that the famous company had just taken on a new contract with the Gas Board to service all their water heaters in South London, they needed to train good men and get them on the road as soon as possible. The wages were good and a van and tools was supplied. As soon as I filled in the application form, and they knew that I had done servicing with vacuum cleaners they were happy to book me for their training course.

Strangely, when I went back to that newspaper to point out the advertisement to Audrey, I couldn't find it. "I know it was here in deep black letters" I pleaded. And then I found it, and it was just printed like all the others, there was nothing to distinguish it from any other advertisement.

I was most thankful to stop being a tally man come debt collector, but my prayers were a little mixed up. Was this what God had for me? I could not work out any divine guidance here, and decided to just go along with things and see where they might lead, after all I was getting a better job.

I was now dealing with gas and water, not electricity. But the course was not too difficult, learning the principles and how to service and repair all the companies range of water heaters, I felt fairly confident at the end of the course.

Each day now I was going into business premises, factories, and private homes servicing water heaters. There were times when repairs and spares were done, and sometimes emergency calls because they were not working quite up to standard. My hours were 9 to 5-30, and my spare time seemed well occupied because I had not had much time to spare in my past job, and it was good to have some time with Audrey. As far as the Ministry was concerned, I felt almost rebellious. Just because I had my evenings free it did not mean that this was God calling me to start studying; I needed more proof that God was calling than this new job; and I told my Minister so. He seemed to take the same attitude as I had imagined from God .. 'Ah! you just wait and see'. I was not quite so keen on a call to the Ministry now, it would involve giving up a lot and living a life with the kind of faith I was not sure I possessed.

I had been working with the new firm for two or three months when one Monday, I was given a call to service the big heater in a large empty house which was about to be occupied. I picked up the key from the estate agent, as instructed, and let myself in. The empty house smelled of new paint and echoed to my every foot step as I discovered the heater down in the basement.

I set to, stripping it down and checking it at each stage. As I did so I was singing what we had sung in the choir the previous day. "We praise Thee O God, we acknowledge Thee to be The Lord.." I was really enjoying myself. It was an empty house so it didn't matter that I was singing lustily!

I paused in my singing as I continued to reassemble. Then I got a shock, I was suddenly aware that I was not alone. Someone was standing somewhere behind me. I went cold all over, and turned, to see three men standing in the shadows. "It's all right". It was the Welsh voice of my area supervisor. "Thought you were running the Eisteddfod down here". They all three came forward and he introduced the other two men, both part of the management.

"Just stand aside will you". The voice seemed kindly. One of the men moved to the heater and made a detailed examination of my work, and I was hoping that it was all right. Finally he nodded to the others and I was allowed to finish the job.

"Right now, if you've finished let us all go and have a drink". I wondered how I was going to get out of this one. "I'm sorry, I don't drink". He looked at me with half a smile "Don't drink tea"? Turning to one of the others he continued "Always thinking we frequent pubs some of them". Within a few minutes we were in a nearby cafe with tea and cake. And I wondering what this was all about.

As if he had read my thoughts.. "You'll be wondering what all this is about. shall I tell him or you Sir?" Between them they now explained that they required one of the engineers to be a local supervisor and had chosen me. I would be required to do my normal morning's work, but be home by 12-30 each day. If any of the engineers had problems or got stuck on the job they would phone me after that time, and it would be my job to see the work done and the man helped. If you get a call for help at five in the afternoon we would expect you to see it through even if it took half the night. Most of the time you will be doing nothing but wait for calls every afternoon.

Over the cuppa we sorted all the details out, and I was to be paid a little extra. From then onward I left as usual for work each morning but was home for lunch with nothing else to do most days except stay near the phone. As I prayed that day I knew what My Lord was saying. It was firmly fixed in my mind. I opened my Bible at random and read from John's Gospel "You have not chosen Me, But I Have chosen You..."

I knew the call of God that day, and it was repeated again and again each day just so that I would really know. I called on my Minister and asked what I should study.

Straight away I made an application, with referees and all other requirements, to be accepted for study for the Congregational Ministry under 'List.B'. There were two lists of clergy. 'List A' were those who had been fully trained through a Congregational College, and ordained as such. List B were those who were unable to do a college course and had done the work without going to college and had taken and passed examinations and the approval board, being ordained as Pastors.

I was duly summoned to appear before the Ministerial Committee in London in September 1955. They saw me, questioned me, but did not considered that I would be a suitable person to be considered for training for the Congregational Ministry.

My Minister contacted Paton Congregational College in Nottingham, and I was set certain tests in English, General Knowledge, and The Bible. I obtain reasonable marks. I was advised just what books to read and what work to do, and my work was checked and marked by the college. I wrote again to be seen by the Ministerial Committee, but they could find no reason to reconsider their opinion'.

The Principal of the college then wrote and invited me to see him in Nottingham, naming a suitable date. This came at a very bad time for I had no money to pay the fares. I went at once to The Lord with the letter. "Dear Lord if You want me to go You must supply the money". When I came to the front door the next morning there on the mat was an envelope. Who had put it through the letter box I did not know and no one knew of my need for fares to Nottingham. I opened it and it contained money. Just enough for the rail fare, and a little over. I never found out who sent it.

I journeyed to Nottingham. When I came out of the station I discovered that there was a bus strike and the college was a long way away. I went to a taxi standing in the rank, and asked if he knew the college, he did, I asked how much to take me. I had enough and one shilling to spare, I went by taxi.

The Principal gave me lunch and we talked quite a bit. His final advise was "You know that you are called of God so nothing and no one can stand in your way. be patient, work hard, God will see you through". He was saying goodbye, and I was wondering how I was going to get back to town, it would take over an hour to walk I thought and I had to catch a train.

"Maurice" called his wife "You simply must go to so and so and see so and so. and you could take Mr Gossage with you".

The Principal drove me to the station. I bought a bar of chocolate to stave off the hunger on the way home and arrived home with six pence in my pocket. The Lord seemed to say "I shall supply all your need". With a little left over!

One of the things suggested to me by the College Principal was that it would help my case considerably, both with the Ministerial Committee and the College Committee, if I could obtain some recognised academic standard like General Certificate of Education (GCE). I though that this was a good idea, although I thought that only school children could take such examinations. I took this idea to my Minister and he arranged for me to study English Language, and English Literature.

Now each day I was working not only on papers set by Paton College, but also work for my G.C.Es. I did however feel guilty that much of this study was being done in my employers time, in the afternoons. I spoke to my Welsh Area Supervisor.

"On average I am only being called out once or sometimes twice a week, it does not seem fair to the firm". He gave me a strange look "It's a good chapel man I can see you are, boy, but you know your trouble?.. You worry too much". On another occasion when talking things over I mentioned my 'free' afternoons, and he replied "We know exactly what you are doing, and you are helping many of these men to become good engineers, in fact it's MY job you'll be after next".

So I was fast becoming an academic .Reading "Northanger Abbey" for Literature, the "Eight parts of speech" for English Language and writing Precis etc for the college. At first my mind would not take it in and I became disheartened, but as I pushed myself I found the work becoming a little easier.

On a cold Wintry November day in 1956 I arrived at a school to take my GCE . I found some difficulty in sitting in the child size desk, and felt great embarrassment as a thirty-two year old man sitting with a class room of children; but when time was called I set to work, finishing my paper in good time. I subsequently received my Pass Certificate.

I now started to study New Testament Greek. and wrote again to the London Moderator for another interview with the Ministerial Committee, following it with several phone calls. I knew what God wanted me to do and I was determined to make others aware of it as well.

There was a new Moderator, Rev. William Simpson. He wasted no time in asking me to see him. When at last I sat before his desk he seemed almost cross with me. According to the information he had I had been twice before the Committee and they had considered that I was not a suitable applicant, I must accept their decision and stop phoning and writing, there were other spheres of Christian work I might try. A calm but very purposeful spirit seemed to come over me as I now spoke to him. I sketched in my background story of searching, and that I now KNEW that I was going into the Congregational Ministry. I had worked hard to show my ability to study, others had faith in my call and now the Ministerial Committee must see this too.

There was a silence in the room, he looked away from me to the papers before him, or was he praying? He then looked at me with a long hard look, with a slight smile on my face I returned his gaze. His face slowly broke into a smile. "All right" he smiled "I cannot tell you what the people have said about you in these references that you submitted in you application, but let me ask you about the Baptist Minister".

I told him of our work together in the war days and his great help and recommendation to the Baptist College.

"Let us start a whole new application. Fill in a new form with the work that you are doing. and supply new referees, and I advise you leave out this Baptist Minister. I took his advise, but wondered about the Baptist Minister. Years later I was to learn that he had confused me with a friend of mine, and had written that I was not a suitable candidate.

The new application now went forward. Churches that I had preached in had special church meetings to recommend me. Ministers and church people wrote of my suitability. My own church in Sydenham wrote a special letter as did the new Minister who had replaced Rev R.W.Carr. When all this reached the Moderator he wrote that I was to come before the Ministerial Committee meeting on April 12th. On April 15th I received the letter giving the committee's decision. They were very happy to recommend that I proceed to apply to Paton College. They were not prepared for me to study at home under the 'list B' method, I had to be List A man and go to College. But how could I go to Nottingham with a wife and child to keep?

The College Principal arranged that I should take the College entrance exams, and appear before the College and University committee on the second and third of July, all meals and hospitality provided.

When I arrived, there were seven other candidates with me, all of us were mature students, and most of us found the exams tough. The examinations also included a medical exam which I feared most of all, but happily those fears proved groundless. Finally the ordeal was over and six of us were accepted to start our college course on October 9th.

The Big Problem now was that I had acquired a habit of eating, and to do that required money, College fees would have to be paid, books purchased, and when those small matters were settled it would be nice if my wife, small daughter and I did not have to sleep with the pigeons in Nottingham Town Square.

The Church in the Grove Congregational Church in Sydenham rejoiced in the news that one of their members had been accepted as a candidate for the Ministry. They did more than that, they called a special Church Meeting and voted a little financial support. It was as much as they could do, but some felt that they would like to have made it more and banded together in an anonymous group pledged to raise an additional annual amount to support this brave family who were going to the wilds of the Midlands.

I was advised of certain charities who might make a grant, and duly wrote a number of letters. All replied but only one favourably, offering a grant of £50 per year for the four years course. The Principal was working hard to provide opportunities for me to obtain a Student Pastorate. One in Coventry seemed to be very hopeful when I visited there to preach with a view to being their student pastor, but a retired man offered to help them out so it all fell through. One by one the schemes fell through. And time was getting short.

Problems that seemed mountainous at first dwindled as prayerful answers came. Like the list of books I would require for the first year; At first it seemed a very expensive list, and I would not be able to buy them, but various clergy found this one and that, someone bought one new, another sent a book token. In no time the problem was gone.

My work at the water heating company was planned several weeks ahead, and I wanted to give them as much time as possible to rearrange their work plans. I wrote and explained my situation and gave them the probable date of leaving. I was taking a risk, as they might have made me leave earlier or made my stay difficult: as it turned out they appreciated my frankness and said they would miss my cheerful approach to their work.

Audrey was ready to go out to work and help me through college, but it was difficult to see what we could do with our three year old. September came and there was no sign of where to live, or where Audrey might be able to work, or what might become of Barbara during the time if her Mum was working.

The wife of the new Minister of our home church had her parents living in Nottingham and they kindly offered to accommodate us for a couple of nights so that Audrey and I could look for accommodation and work. Friends looked after Barbara, and so off we went.

The College Principal's wife spent the whole day on the phone for us, while we trudged the streets of Nottingham in the rain stopping regularly to find our way from a wet bedraggled map of the city. Through the influence and efforts of the principal's wife we solved one problem. There was only one post open, that of School Secretary in a Junior school; during the interview Audrey managed to work out that little Barbara could be in the pre school nursery during the school hours that she worked.

There was only one condition that we were unhappy about. Audrey had to be resident in the City area, not the County. With more confidence than we felt we told them that we would be living in the City area, and would send our address on.

As we tramped the city for accommodation we heard again and again "No Rooms to let, sorry". or "No children". or "Four guineas (or more) a week". We returned to Sydenham with this problem still unsolved. Where would we live?

We were starting the last week of my work, we still did not know whether we would be going or not, we could not go without somewhere to live. It was coming to the nail-biting finish, and our faith was being tested to the full.

I phoned Nottingham to ask whether there was any hope of accommodation yet. "I suppose that you would be happy to go into a temporary accommodation until something else comes"? "Whatever you advise". I replied. "I will keep trying!" was the reply.

Only a few days to go and the phone rang, it was the Principal. "One of the students who will be in your first year with you has managed to get three rooms; He and his wife are happy to offer you one room as a bed sitting room for the three of you, you can share the kitchen, will you go there?" Rather than miss the opening of the college course and Audrey's job I said 'yes'.

Armed with a large trunk and various cases, Audrey, Barbara and I were seen off at the station by friends from the church. We had boarded the train for Nottingham. I was on my way to college, and in four years, if I could get through the course, I would be a Minister, living in The Manse of one of our many churches. I thanked God. But Those four years represented a very long way to go yet.

My resources were nil, could God? Would God supply all our needs?

Chapter 13.

Arriving in Nottingham, there was no way we could get our trunk and cases plus the three of us to a place called Elm Avenue without a taxi, so we arrived in style at the home of Tom and Molly, and were shown to our one room where we would settle in until something better might come our way. They were very kind, and laid on a hot lunch for us.

Soon Audrey and Barbara were catching the morning bus across the city to the school where Audrey would work and three year old Barbara would start nursery school; while Tom and I caught the bus to College. When we met together in the evening Audrey had obviously felt the strain of the new work, Barbara had not settled in very well to this strange life of strange people, and I felt it wise not to share much of my first day.

Tom and Molly were from Holland, with continental ways, which may have accounted for our bed cover; It was a quilt which was like a large bag filled with feathers, this had two temperatures: Freezing if you push it off, Sweltering if you put it on. Each night we tossed and turned, and each night Barbara was sick in her cot. There was little sleep for any of us after that with all the strange sounds of an unfamiliar city.

For Audrey and Barbara the second day was like the first except worse, for they were both so tired. For me I began to understand the regimentation of college life. The first year men had certain duties, like laying the lunch table, and ringing the bell to signal the beginning and ending of sessions; and of course we had our lectures, with copious notes to take for each subject.

If you wonder just what theological students have to study here is a brief list of some of the subjects. Miss the paragraph out if you are not interested!

The Atonement.

The Gospels.

Literature of the Old Testament.
and of the New Testament.
Biblical Archaeology.

Prophecy and prophets.

Messianic ideas in the Old Testament.

Practical problems in the Ministry.

The Bible.

Philosophical Theology.

The educational system.

Elocution.

The origin of religion.

Christian sociology.

Greek.

Political theory.

History of the Hebrew people.

Theology.

Homiletics.

Church History.

Christian apologetics.

Psychology.

Economic history.

The History of Nonconformity.

Society and social administration.

Pastoral psychology.

Comparative Religion.

English.

Logic.

The Church, Ministry, and Sacraments.

Congregational History.
and English History

And there were others.

That night we continued our fight with what we now called our Barrage Balloon, and Barbara was sick again. In fact, sadly she was sick every night for the first four weeks we were there.

We first year students were welcomed into the student body and spent one afternoon being initiated. All part of the college tradition. The pattern of life was lectures in the mornings at college or the university, lunch at college, and afternoons and evenings for study and week end preparation of services and sermons. Except for Thursday evenings when there was a lecture in the City on English history.

After two weeks I caught influenza, and stayed in bed with a raging temperature, and no one to do anything for me. I then got a series of nose bleedings which I could not stop, neither could the local doctor. I ended up in the hospital having cauterization of the little veins in the nose, and was sent back to our one room and told not to bend or move for several days until the nose had a chance to heal.

About five weeks or so after coming to Nottingham I was able to preach at a little local church. I returned successfully without a nose bleeding. but feeling very depressed. Barbara was asleep in her cot, so Audrey and I had to whisper. I told Audrey that I was no longer sure that God had called me. I felt that somehow I had misread the signals. I could not bear to see her so tired and see Barbara so upset. I had hardly seen the college, and felt weak and tired. I was about ready to go back to living in with my parents again and try to get my old job back.

Audrey said that if only we had a place of our own we could build a life for ourselves for the four years. "Tomorrow" she said "Starts our half term holiday week, let us call on all the estate agents, and try to get somewhere to live. We will ask The Lord that if He wants you in the Ministry He will find us somewhere to live." "If we have not found something by the end of the week we can make plans to go back to Sydenham."

With this prayer and resolve we went to bed and slept soundly for the first time since we had been there. And Barbara was not sick. We slept late, and awoke around nine to find the College Principal at the front door. Happily he said "I won't come in Gerald, but I would like you to come to the college early this afternoon, I think I just might have somewhere for you to live."

We had a leisurely breakfast and relaxing, we played and had a bit of fun with Barbara; then all three of us went to the college, to the principal's apartment.

He was trying to reach someone by phone and it took some considerable time. At last he said "Come along, I will take you there and introduce you to this estate agent." We met the agent who led the way in his car with us following. Down the kind of little back streets I had never seen before we finally reaching the Radford district of the city.

We stopped outside an empty three story house in a small cobbled street. The house was built straight on to the pavement with no front garden or yard.

The agent opened the door and we stepped straight into the small front room. From there we then passed by the stairs to continue into a small living room. Then down two steps to a kitchen. The toilet, we were told was at the bottom of the back yard.

Up stairs were two bedrooms on one floor, and one on the top floor. The whole house had been painted in a light green colour, and looked clean as far as decorations were concerned.

We had a further look around peering in cupboards. The gas and electricity meters were in a cellar below the living room we were told.

"What do you think"? asked the Principal. "Very nice" we replied. We were back on the pavement. "Is there somewhere we could sign up"? the agent was keen to get on. The Principal said that the owner of a greengrocer shop in the next street attended one of our churches, perhaps we could go there. We drove round to the end of the next cobbled street.

The Principal went into the shop to ask if we might use his back room, and we all trooped in.

The agent seated himself at the table and prepared a rent book; we sat around uncertainly. "What is the rent?" I asked. he told me. It was just about five shillings a week more than I had decided was my top price. He looked up from the rent book. "You know that there is fifty pounds to pay.. for the decorations" he said casually. This was a kind of key money often charged in those days of housing shortage.

I knew that I would not have fifty shillings after paying two weeks rent in advance. What ever could I do?

I looked at the Principal. he gave a little smile and looked away. I looked at Audrey, she shrugged her shoulders, I looked across to the greengrocer who was doing his books at a roll-top desk in the corner, he looked back at me and raised his eyebrows, leaning over he whispered "Haven't you got it"? "No!" "Could you pay it off in weekly instalments"?

"Y.. yes" I said uncertainly and not wholly truthfully.

He reached for his cheque book and wrote. "Who do you want it paid to"? he addressed the agent. The cheque passed between them, and I said thank you. Within minutes we were out on the pavement again, I felt numb and bewildered as I said goodbye to the agent. My hand held the keys of the house and rent book, I held them up for Audrey to see, "When The Lord answers prayer He doesn't mess about does He?" I whispered.

We were driven home; and it was only then that Audrey and I looked at each other. "The Lord's express delivery". she commented; then we laughed and all three hugged each other. Then we thanked The Lord.

I went out to phone home and give them the good news, also to arrange for our bits and pieces to be delivered to the new home by Thursday.

It was while we were having tea that Audrey dropped the bombshell. "We have sent for our bits of furniture, but we haven't any floor covering, that all belongs to your mother. And I have nothing to put up at the windows for curtains. What are we going to do?" I grinned "Pray?". "I suppose we shall have to, I don't know any other way".

The prayer was sent "Dear Lord, You know what we want, floor coverings and curtains, please, will You?".

"There is something else we need" I said facetiously "To know where the house is! Did you notice the road or the number?" "9, Byfield Street, It's on that rent book you were waving about" grinned Audrey.

When we had been in Sydenham we had bought a few bits of second hand furniture in preparation for the day we might get housed, and it would now arrive on Thursday; In whispered conversation, so that we did not disturb sleeping Barbara, we planned where each piece might go. Then headed for bed, happier than we had been for a very long time.

We awoke to the postman's knock, and I opened a letter with a post mark I did not recognise. Out came a letter and a cheque. I read the letter to Audrey "You will not remember me I think, but you preached at our church, and told us of your hopes to enter college for the Ministry. I phoned your home and your mother gave me your address. I decided to write, and The Lord seemed to be saying that I should send you a gift with the letter, so please find the enclosed cheque to help out with any need that you may have, or you might buy some books you need. " Audrey and I danced around in circles, "The Lord has sent the floor coverings and curtains" we sang.

What a day that Tuesday was. We borrowed a tape measure and measured up the house for window curtains and linoleum for the floor. The greengrocer cashed the cheque for us, and we arranged to pay off his generous loan; then we went out shopping to start equipping the new home.

We just could not believe that we had A House! Accommodation of any kind was almost impossible to come by at that time. A flat or rooms would have cost us more than the rent of this house. We wondered just how The Lord could have done it.

All that we could learn about the house was that the owner had redecorated it and put it up for sale, people said that it had not sold because there were foreign people living next door, so the owner had let it. But that still left many questions unanswered. All we knew was that we had witnessed the biggest miracle we had ever seen. We discovered that the living room floor was most uneven. so we started to explore why and discovered that in places there were as many as twenty-three different layers of linoleum. in other places not so many. We scraped the whole lot off, ready for our new floor covering to go down.

By Thursday, when our furniture arrived the house was clean from top to bottom, with curtains at the windows and floors covered. That night we slept soundly in our own beds, and in our Nottingham home, a home that we could not get anywhere else. A home that only Our God could make possible.

As the months went by the top bedroom became my study. It housed my home-made desk, bookshelves, and a couple of chairs.

When Basil and June, two of our home church friends came up to visit us, he, being an electrical wizard managed to convert two old radio sets into a wonderful intercom system whereby I could speak and listen from my top study through speakers, one behind the front door in the lounge, and another in the living room.

This meant Audrey and I could talk to each other when I was up in the study working, and she down stairs. It also enabled me to reply to anyone knocking on the front door without coming down from the top of the house.

Fellow students calling round could be told to come in and come up; and when the man came to read the meter I could tell him to push the door it was open, direct him to the living room, and then switch to the other speaker and tell him where the door was for the cellar. I enjoyed that! He thought we were mad!

I had early on discovered the reality of the bible verse which says "My God shall supply all your needs according to His riches in glory, in Christ Jesus". We now used this again and again. Whenever we had a need we just asked and it came. Usually, as Audrey had said 'The Lord's Express delivery'.

The reality of His presence was something we both discovered in practical terms. I was forced to learn at such a rate that it would have been quite impossible if I could not turn to The Lord and whisper "I don't get this Lord let me understand". And understanding would come. "Lord I'm tired tonight and I have to prepare for Sunday what am I to say?" My mind would have a flash of inspiration, I would feel wide awake while I scribbled my sermon notes, then tiredness would sweep over me and I would tumble into bed.

When we needed more income, The Lord provided me with a Student Pastorate at Albion Congregational Church in the city. There we began to collect many new friends, and the friendships were as pure gold to us. The years went by slowly, but every moment of every day seemed to be filled to overflowing.

Just how the finances came I just cannot recall. I mowed lawns to pay for college fees, took jobs as postman during the Christmas vacations, worked at the Boots Chemist factory in the summer, preached, and lectured.

In our third year we experienced what we thought would be an absolute disaster, without anyway out.

Audrey and I had taken every precaution that we should not increase our family before getting into the full time ministry. We were shocked then to discover that Audrey was expecting our second child.

We were relying on her income at the school. If she stopped, the income stopped, and I would not be able to do my final year, or stay in Nottingham.

It was one thing to ask The Lord for a pair of shoes for Barbara and expect to receive them. We could understand how He could touch people, and circumstances for that kind of request, but why had this happened. We could do no other than commit our way to The Lord and believe that He knew what He was doing.

As the months went by we found it difficult to maintain our faith. It must have been Satan that kept at us with suggestions that it was pointless working at college as I would not be there long. That we could not stay in Nottingham for there would be no money soon for the rent. I asked that The Lord would help us keep our faith in Him. Audrey began to feel uncomfortable in the evenings sitting on the only chairs we had, she remarked one day that she could use a better chair, her back hurt. She went upstairs to lay down, it was a Saturday afternoon. I went out, heading for a shop for something.

In the next street there was a hall, and as I now passed it I noticed that they were holding a jumble sale in aid of some charity. I looked in at the doorway and saw an armchair, and my mind went at once to Audrey's need. I stepped in and looked.

Someone came up to ask for threepence to come in. Some one else called out "don't charge now we are near to closing". There were two matching armchairs and on one there was in chalk a price of seven shillings and sixpence.

I ran back to the house and got Audrey round to look at these two chairs. At seven shillings and six pence each I commented, if they will sell one we could have a very real bargain.

I could see that Audrey liked them. A man approached us "Good chairs those". We hesitated wondering just whether we could buy just one. The man misunderstood our hesitation "All right" he smiled "Five shillings" I looked at Audrey, again he misunderstood our hesitation "Half a crown" He smiled.

I handed him a ten shilling note, "We'll have both" expecting five shillings change. He gave me seven and six pence. He was selling them at two shillings and six pence The Pair!

In spite of her condition, Audrey picked up one and I the other and we carried them home. We had those chairs for years, the most comfortable chairs we ever had.

On Monday I had the day free to study and was working away when there came down the road a man with a barrow calling out for Rags Bottles and Bones!. I called to him from my top window, and raced down to the cellar where I had seen a quantity of old lead water piping laying among the rubbish. I offer this to the man. "A pound governor!" he said. Then looking into my face his face seemed to change "No, it's got to be One pound two and six to you sir". He paid me, took the lead and was gone.

I had the cost to the chairs and a pound note. My faith suddenly returned in strength. It was the way that man had looked at me and raised the payment. It may seem silly, but to me at that moment God was saying I can supply your EVERY need, pay for comfortable chairs and leave twice what you had before.

My sermon that coming Sunday was of Christ feeding five thousand men and there being twelve basket full of scraps left over. I knew what I was talking about from experience!

The time was getting near for the biggest miracle of them all if He was going to keep me at college for my final year.

In typical human fashion Audrey worked out what we must do now that she must leave the school and prepare for the baby.

Christmas was coming. Audrey would finish at the end of that school term. We would enjoy our last Christmas in Nottingham, and then move back to my parents home in early January where I would try to get my old job back.

The days were tinged with not a little sadness, we had come so far and achieved so much. For three years we had made it, now, to be piped at the post for the lack of one year. But we could see no possible way that Audrey's income could be replaced when Audrey was no longer at work and I in college. There was no way out of this one. Although we would not voice it, we could not see how even The Lord God could deal with this situation.

I was not a brilliant student. The end of term and end of year examinations had shown that I only just got through to the next, and I now began to wonder if I would indeed make the grade at the close of this term examinations. It had been the toughest term's work, and it was demanding every thing I had to keep up with the others. If I didn't pass I would be out, if I did pass I would be out it seemed. It was proving hard to believe that there could be any possible solution.

It did not help one afternoon when I got home to discover that I had left the books I needed for study in the college library. I journeyed all the way back, walked into the library and there they were, just where I had left them.

As I passed the Principal's office he came out. "Ah! The very man I want". he called "I have three ladies in my office that I would like you to meet". I did not want to meet ladies, I wanted to go home and work. He mumbled something about not knowing where God may lead, as he ushered me in to their presence.

We were introduced, and between them the story of why they had come was told. They belonged to a temperance society, They and a committee of ladies had been shocked that so many young people had nowhere to meet in the evenings and that they were drifting into the pubs. The ladies had decided to do something about it, and had purchased a large disused billiard hall, got rid of the billiard tables, cleaned it up and set it up as a youth club.

Because their organization had a youth department called The Guild of Abstaining Youth, the letters G.A.Y. had caused them to name the place The Gay Youth Centre. (This was long before the word 'gay' had other meanings of course.)

They were now experiencing hundreds of young people crowding in each night, and the ladies were frightened of the leather-jacketed, flick knife possessing youngsters and they wanted a man about the place. The only rule of the place was that once they paid to come in, they stayed in for the evening and did not leave for the pubs. But now each evening the ladies were locked in their canteen, afraid to come out. Could one of the students come and help out for three nights a week?

"You could help these ladies" smiled the Principal. I made a feeble remark about my future not being too sure, but before I knew what hit me, I was committed to help them out.

I found the hall, and spent an evening walking around and talking to the young people as best I could. They had a Juke box blaring out the latest hits, which made conversation difficult. Over three hundred young people were there, drinking endless coke, and either playing table tennis and darts etc or just talking.

On the third night that I was there I was surprised to see three well dressed men come in. They asked me if I were in charged and I said yes. They introduced themselves as from the County Youth Department and asked a lot of questions about the numbers attending and what we were seeking to achieve. Then they left.

I had not expected the letter I received from them a few days later. It said that if I filled in the enclosed form giving my qualifications for being in leadership, and I was prepared to do four evenings a week I might qualify as a paid Youth Leader.

I showed the letter to the ladies in charge who urged me to send in the form. I checked it with the Principal who advised me to put on the form all the subjects I was studying and return it. To my amazement I had a letter back confirming that I was recognised as a part time youth leader and the salary was even larger than Audrey had received from her work as School Secretary.

He had done it! We could stay in Nottingham. I obtained a good pass mark in the college exams', I could remain on at college. We always knew by faith that there was nothing He could not do, now we had seen it for ourselves.

My fourth and final year meant that I could no longer have a student pastorate. I started to travel each Sunday to churches, sometimes difficult to reach. My skin disease was playing me up, and I found that I could not do much walking.

Trudging along from the nearest bus stop one Sunday I felt the rubbing of my trousers against my inner leg, red and raw. Soon I was bleeding, and I arrived at the church putting a brave smile on, but heading for the toilet in order to remove my trousers and stem the blood. It was a rough day, and I felt that I did not do my best. I returned to find the same problem on the homeward journey. I prayed as I hobbled along "Dear Lord, can you solve this problem".

On Monday morning I had the morning free and just had to catch a bus into town. Getting to the main road I noticed as I was passing a small one-man garage that there was a car outside with a white painted price on the windscreen £5. I knew this could not possibly be right but I went in. The man pulled himself from under a car, and I asked him about the black Morris 8 outside labelled five pounds. "Blooming kids". he came back "They are always doing things like this; of course it's not five pounds". He asked me if I were looking for a car. I told him I was looking for one to use just on Sundays and this so intrigued him he asked what I wanted it for.

I told the friendly garage man that I was in my final year of training for the Ministry and that on health grounds I was finding it difficult to get to churches to preach on Sundays.

"Look" he said "That car is just a nuisance to me. I have three cars waiting for servicing and jobs to be done and I can't get them in because that Morris is taking up the only space I have. If I park a car in the road they fine me. I'll do a deal with you. You take that car and park it outside your house, and you can drive it to your church on Sunday."

I reminded him that it would not get sold standing outside my house. He said "If I get a customer for it or want it I know where to come and get it". He fixed me up with car insurance, and I got into the car and drove it first to the city and then back home. Where it stood outside until I needed it on Sunday.

I drove to my preaching appointment on Sunday feeling much better for doing so. Thanking The Lord again, and returned the car on Monday. There was no where to park it. I parked it in the road while I went in to ask where he might like it put. "Outside your house so that you can use it next Sunday" was his reply. There was nowhere else to put it. So home it came again.

After this had gone on for several weeks I went to have a talk with him. "I can not just take advantage of your generosity every week, I must pay you something toward depreciation, tax and things". He finally accepted the pound I offered.

Now each week I reserved a little of my preaching fee for the garage man, and he wrote down every penny I gave him on a piece of paper which he kept in the car log book. One week I told him that I would not want it as I was going to London to visit my Mother, and old friends, preaching at my home church. "Take the car man!" he smiled "I have still no place to put it here"

What a joy it was to drive Audrey and Barbara to Sydenham and back. It was good not to have to fuss with trains.

On the morning of the ninth of March Audrey had me call the midwife. Who came, and went away saying "Plenty of time yet" She left me to fuss, and run up and down stairs. Then the baby was coming, I rushed into the street and there she was sauntering along. She was only just in time for the performance, scaring the life out of me by returning to the house just four minutes before the baby arrived.

"You have a son" she called down; Peter David was born. and I knelt by the chair and thanked Our Father, offering this new life to The Glory of God. Asking that one day he would become a Christian and serve Christ all his days.

It was time for me to think and pray about which would be my first church as a Fulltime Minister. I had several invitations to various churches, but I waited for guidance.

It soon came. Belvedere Congregational Church just on the borders of London and Kent wrote for me to visit them with a view to Ministry. Before going into college I had helped them out when their Minister had been taken ill just prior to a Harvest service. Then, they had expressed great pleasure with what I was able to do. Now that Minister had retired, they wanted me to be their new Minister. The Lord seemed to draw me to them. A weekend spent with them confirmed that this was where Our Lord was calling me. I wrote to accept their unanimous call.

Their previous Minister had retired after twenty-nine years with them, and he had owned his own house. They therefore did not have a Manse for us to live in, but now they started house hunting. As July edged ever nearer the excitement of the future infected all of us in the leaving year. I was busy arranging the greatest day of my life, when I would be recognised and set aside as a Man Of God and Ordained into the Christian Ministry.

Audrey and I wondered what the new Manse would be like and what the future would hold for us.

The church found a suitable house in nearby Bexleyheath. Audrey and I went to see it, a semi detached house which would be our new home, The Manse for us to live in. Once more the Morris eight did the journey and the man at the garage seemed as pleased at our news as we were.

The college chapter of our life was closing with final things. The final exams, the final 'binge', an occasion when all the other students treat the leaving year to a dinner, the final Valedictory Service, and the final goodbyes. The last few days in what had been our Nottingham home, and the arrangements for our removal from the little cobbled street of Byfield Street to Belvedere.

The final drive to the good garage man who had helped me so much with his generous loan of that car. I thanked the man warmly for his friendship and great kindness. I offered my final gift of money from the last preaching fee.

His face was straight and expressionless. Slowly he walked to where he kept the list of payments and Log book, brought it over and placed the Log Book in my hands. "Don't forget to put the address of that new Manse in the log book before you register your self as the new owner". he said still with a poker face. "I've really no room to keep it here you know, and it's a long road to the Manse, lad".

Printed in the United Kingdom
by Lightning Source UK Ltd.
123293UK00002B/199-207/A

9 781425 958008